Praise for *Coaching*

'A unique and valuable adjunct to coaching literature ~~for~~ ~~~~
agers and leaders.'

Dr Jayne Chidgey-Clark

'There is growing evidence for the benefits of working in and with nature in the field of human development. This timely book offers a comprehensive guide to coaching outdoors, from contract through to completion. Packed with vignettes and suggestions, it supports the coach to invite nature to enhance their practice.'

Professor Charlotte Sills

'This book is an expression of everything that is Lesley; a remarkable, dedicated woman. She is a challenging, provocative facilitator of growth and learning. A lover of nature and the outdoors with a brave heart whose capacity allows her to take others to their edge. She has unfolded all of this through her writing for you to unlock your potential to coach with nature.'

Sue Knight, NLP Master Trainer and Author of *NLP at Work*

'If you even needed confirmation that coaching outdoors provided tangible, measurable outcomes, this book gives you just that, along with practical suggestions on "how to". Great advice for coaches and organisations.'

Alysoun Sturt-Scobie, Human Resource Practitioner, Coach and Mediator

'*Coaching Outdoors* is groundbreaking. It lands the whole outdoor coaching concept for coaches and line managers alike. The gravitas of what *Coaching Outdoors* can offer is found not only through the evidence and stories shared, but through the personal journey the reader takes when they engage in each of the beautifully crafted activities.'

Barry Chamberlain, CEO

'Highly practical, well researched and beautifully written. Ideal for anyone wishing to take coaching conversations outdoors for the first time, or to deepen their existing outdoor coaching practice. The author's depth of knowledge is clear and authentic. She role models coaching in what she offers to the reader.'

Sam Eddleston, Clear Focus Coaching & Development

'Lesley demonstrates the compelling rationale for outdoor coaching through combining empirical evidence with personal experience and testimonials. The practical tips, advice and exercises make it a very useful resource for those wanting to take their coaching conversations outdoors. The book is authentic; I love the way Lesley's energy and enthusiasm are translated into text – not easy to do! The sharing of personal experiences adds a further degree of texture.'

Professor Neil Guha, Nottingham University

'A wonderful unique and thought-provoking resource for anyone interested in taking coaching conversations outdoors. Lesley writes with an engaging informality that speaks to the reader and makes this an easy read. *Coaching Outdoors* is packed with research, useful information, coaching methods and real-life examples. The layout is clear and accessible and it is so helpful to have many different strands gathered together in one place. This will be invaluable for so many people. It is exactly what has been needed in the outdoor coaching space.'

Hannah Vertigen, Coach, Clear Air Coaching

'*Coaching Outdoors* is a wonderful toolkit of the best ideas, experiences and research I've come across to help us invite nature into our coaching conversations whilst also appreciating and nurturing our planet. It's beautifully written by Lesley, whose passion and expertise in this area come through in the evocative and insightful vignettes, provocations and activities to support both the coach and coachee. Whether you are a professional coach, just starting on the coaching journey, a line manager or want to coach yourself, I highly recommend this book.'

Sam Clarke, Coach and Trainer, Believe in You Ltd

'This book is rich and comprehensive, leaving no stone unturned. Lesley has a lovely easy readable style coupled with a great structure which is simple and easy to follow. She uses descriptions and stories which bring examples to life and really provoke the imagination.'

Helen Daniel, Coach

COACHING OUTDOORS

THE ESSENTIAL GUIDE TO PARTNERING WITH NATURE IN YOUR COACHING CONVERSATIONS

LESLEY ROBERTS

First published in Great Britain by Practical Inspiration Publishing, 2022

ISBN   9781788603423   (print)
       9781788603447   (epub)
       9781788603430   (mobi)

Cover image by Jack Skinner, @jack_skinner

Photographs by Lesley Roberts or taken with gratitude from Unsplash

Figure design by Lauri King

Every effort has been made to trace copyright holders and to obtain their permission for the use of copyright material. The publisher apologizes for any errors or omissions and would be grateful if notified of any corrections that should be incorporated in future reprints or editions of this book.

Want to bulk-buy copies of this book for your team and colleagues? We can introduce case studies, customize the content and co-brand *Coaching Outdoors* to suit your business's needs.

Please email info@practicalinspiration.com for more details.

Practical Inspiration Publishing

MIX
Paper | Supporting responsible forestry
FSC   FSC® C013604

For Torrin. Here's Mummy's book. It's not a story book, but if you hunt through the pages, you'll find 'Plop' the owl.

Contents

Foreword by Neil Reynolds (Mars Wrigley) .... *xiii*
My Story .... *xv*
What You Will Find in This Book .... *xxiii*

Section I – Setting the Scene 1
What is Coaching? 3
What is Coaching Outdoors? 7
   Nature-Based Interventions 9
Why is Coaching Outdoors Growing? 15
   The World Today 16
   Demands on Leaders Today 16
   Society Today 17
   Covid-19 Impact 18
   Climate Crisis 19

Section II – The Benefits of Coaching Outdoors 21
Our Systemic Connection with Nature 23
   Evolution 25
   Our Relationship with the Earth 26
Planet Benefits 29
   Pathways to Nature Connectedness 31
   The Coach's Role 32
   Activity – Connect with Nature 33
Wellbeing Benefits 35
   Summary of Research 36
   Prescribing Nature 38
   Benefits of Walking 39

Relevant Theories 41
Activity – Wellbeing Experience 43
Client Benefits 45
Ease and Equality from Being Side by Side 46
Supported Silence Offering Processing Time 47
Clarity of Thinking 48
Creativity 48
Perspective 50
Activity – Client Experience 51
Coach Benefits 53
Key Themes 54
Client Connection 54
In Flow 56
Congruence and Authenticity 58
Bravery 59
Activity 1 – Preparation Ritual 61
Activity 2 – Experience Reflection 61
Organisational Benefits 63
Quality Outputs 64
Resilience 65
Speed of Results 66
Taking Others Along 66
Radical Candour 67

Section III – Get Started Coaching Outdoors **69**
Psychological Safety 71
When Not to Go Outdoors 71
Listening to Intuition 72
Chemistry Sessions 73
Our Past Experiences 74
Location 75
Other Considerations 77
Thoughts to Leave You With 77
Activity – Plan for a Client Session 78
Contracting 79
What's Different About a Contract for Coaching Outdoors? 80
The Best-Laid Plans… 81
Confidentiality 81

Activity – Agreeing a Contract 82
Location, Location, Location 83
Physical Comfort 83
The Right Container 84
Green Space/Blue Space 85
What Makes a Good Location? 85
What About the Travel Time? 87
Unknown Venues 88
Portfolio of Locations 89
Does it Feel Right? 89
Activity – Explore a Location 90
Location Checklist 91
Weather 93
Comfort Zones 93
Windy Weather 96
Warm and Sunny 97
Activity – Your Weather Boundaries 98
Clothing and Kit 99
Clothing 99
Footwear 100
Kit 101
Insurance and Training 103
Supporting Your Client with Their Choices 104
Activity – Explore Location and Kit 105
Give It a Go 107
Activity – Have a Client Session Outdoors and Reflect on It 107

Section IV – Nature and You **109**
Your Nature Connection 111
Activity – Your Relationship with Nature 113
Your Nature Connection Practice 115
Activity – Your Nature Switch Continuum 117
Activity – Commune with Nature 118

Section V – Nature as a Co-Facilitator **121**
What is Nature as a Co-Facilitator? 123
Suggestions for Framing 125
Suggested Exercises – Transference 127

Activity – Your Current Practice 128
Metaphor and Mirror 129
Metaphor 129
Examples of Enquiring Metaphor Questions 133
Suggested Metaphor Exercises 133
Signs 133
Mirror/Parallel Process 135
Suggested Mirror Exercises 137
Becoming Open 138
Constellations 139
Suggested Constellation Questions 140
Activity – What is Nature Offering You? 140
Rhythm and Seasons 141
Nature's Rhythm 141
Seasons 142
Suggested Spring Coaching Questions 145
Suggested Summer Coaching Questions 147
Suggested Autumn Coaching Questions 148
Suggested Winter Coaching Questions 151
The Senses 151
Knowing Yourself 152
Bringing the Seasons Inside 152
Activity – A Sensual Seasonal Walk 153
Trust Your Intuition and Give It a Go 155
Intuition 155
Activity – Go with the Flow 157

Section VI – Teams and Working Remotely 159
Working with Groups and Teams Outdoors 161
The Difference Between Groups and Teams 161
Contracting and Psychological Safety for Teams Outdoors 162
Location Choice 163
Nature as a Co-Facilitator with Teams 163
Reflections from Participants 164
Suggested Team Activities 165
Remote Coaching with Nature 169
The Good Old-Fashioned Phone 169
Indoor Virtual Sessions (e.g. Zoom) 173

Three Exercise Suggestions 173
Creating a Natural Environment Inside 174
Three Types of Outdoor Virtual Sessions 174
Nature Connection Between Sessions 176
Priming Between Sessions 176
Touch Points 177
Activity – Share Your Ideas 177

Section VII – The Future **179**
The Future of Coaching 181
Growth of the Market 181
Accreditation and Regulation 182
Corporate Experience 182
The Need for Return on Investment (ROI) Evaluation 183
Virtual Coaching 183
Coaching Specialisms 184
Future Proof 184
The Future of Coaching Outdoors 185
ROI/Research 185
Contribute 186
Conclusion 187

Appendices *189*
Appendix 1: CoachingOutdoors.com *191*
Appendix 2: Sample Risk Assessment Form *193*
Appendix 3: Resources *195*
Acknowledgements *197*
References *199*
Index *209*

Foreword

WHEN LESLEY FIRST told me that she was planning to write a book based on two of her clearest passions – coaching and the outdoors – I could not think of a better combination of topics nor a better-qualified author to tell the story.

The world of work has been truly transformed in the aftermath of the Covid pandemic with more virtual and less face-to-face working for many of us. When I am lucky enough to meet up with my team or colleagues, I am committed to maximising the impact of our time together. I use many of the lessons I learned from working with Lesley, often switching the office or hotel reception area for a stroll in the park, along the canal or even just a walk to the local coffee shop and back. Lesley has done a superb job collating all her knowledge, experience and research, and that of others, into this essential guide. There are ideas and approaches for teams as well as day-to-day coaching conversations. The book is as accessible for line managers and leaders as it is for coaches. I've personally found some insights that I can take into the virtual meeting space.

I first met Lesley in 2001 working together at Mars. My early memories often involve her pushing to get through the formal agenda as fast as we could to leave the meeting room behind and head out into the grounds for a stroll. Looking back now I can see that those 'walk and talk sessions' were actually enabling the real business or personal development discussions to happen. They built trust, enriched relationships and often helped stimulate new ideas on how to solve a problem. And the best bit was that they didn't feel like 'real work'.

Throughout the next 15 years I was lucky enough to work with Lesley several times as she progressed from commercial leadership roles to ones responsible for people development, executive coaching and team performance. Lesley was the team performance coach for my Sales Leadership Team. I was continually amazed by the power of the sessions she ran for us. Always ensuring we prioritised selecting the right location to allow hard topics to surface in a natural and easy way and enabling team members to be open and ask for help. Being outdoors brought wellbeing and creativity into the mix too. There was undoubtedly a clear helping hand from the environment around us as the sessions were more enjoyable, productive, easier and, in all honesty, less intense than they would have been back in the office.

We are blessed to live in a beautiful world. There are amazing locations for coaching outdoors everywhere and we don't even have to look too far if we take notice of what is around us. Enjoy this book and the multitude of gems that emerge. You'll soon discover your favourite locations, tools and insights. Oh, and if you are in the UK like me, don't forget a coat most of the time…

Neil Reynolds, VP Global Digital Commerce at Mars Wrigley

My Story

Look deep into nature, and then you will understand everything better.

Albert Einstein, 1955

A Chat with a Mountain

IT WAS DECEMBER 1994 and I was on a university club mountaineering trip to the awe-inspiring Glen Coe (long before James Bond ever made it there in *Skyfall*). The weather was beautiful – clear, cold, snowy winter days and starry nights. Early in the week as we climbed Aonach Eagach Ridge, I found myself looking over at Buachaille Etive Mòr – probably Scotland's most iconic mountain. I felt tiny and insignificant in the Buachaille's shadow. I imagined all of the life that it had seen come and go. I quietly, respectfully questioned: '*How long have you been there? What have you seen? How long will you be there after I'm gone?*' I pondered. '*How old is the Earth?*' And in that moment, it became clear to me that what I did in the world really didn't matter as my time here is so short. '*I'm not even an ant's footprint on the time-line of life,*' I thought.

> Were we to reduce… evolution to the span of one year, we left the African Savannah a mere four to five days ago. The first civilizations developed less than a day ago. The scientific revolution clocks in at roughly one hour ago, and the digital revolution in which we are all living represents a few eye blinks.
>
> (Palmer & Crawford, 2013, p.124)

Standing looking at 'the Buachaille', I had just experienced what Totton describes:

As well as the other-than-human, we encounter the *more-than-human*: aspects of reality which are much bigger than we are. These include... rivers and lakes; the sea; mountains; winds; sun, sky and stars. To approach these entities... is to remember the true seriousness and depth of existence, and just how small we are in the face of the universe.

(Totton, 2014, p.15)

That moment in Glen Coe was the first conscious experience I had of being coached by nature (although I wouldn't have known that's what it was at the time).

Finding Purpose

And so began my passion for personal development in nature. In 2006 while studying Neuro-Linguistic Programming (NLP) with Sue Knight, I began to define my purpose further. We were exploring Dilts' (1988) Logical Levels of Change model and my Glen Coe experience became very meaningful again:

The level of purpose is sometimes described as the level of spirituality... What it refers to here are the larger systems of which we are a part. Understanding the spiritual level for ourselves means understanding the interconnections between us and the bigger systems.

(Knight, 1995, p.211)

I realised that my purpose in life is to support people in unlocking their potential, holding the belief that this will have a positive impact for them and others they interact with. The metaphor that came to me was of dropping a pebble in the sea and watching the ripples expand outwards.

Outdoor Development Experience

By the time I started executive coaching, I had years of experience of working with people and groups outdoors. At university I'd majored in Outdoor Education and gone on to teach PE along with running the school residentials and the Duke of Edinburgh Award Scheme. I'd also spent many happy summers working in a variety of outdoor centres. After teaching, I moved to working with youth at risk in the beautiful, powerful and wild Highlands of Scotland in a tiny village called Applecross. Our work was based on experiential learning with cognitive and therapeutic developmental techniques to build skills and unlock confidence. Being in the wilderness, which was an integral part of our programmes, helped those young people gain greater understanding of themselves, how they connected with others and the wider world, leading to lasting positive change.

Theory and Reality

During one of my days off while in Applecross, I went rock climbing and unfortunately took a 30-foot fall, breaking and dislocating my right ankle. I was taken to Inverness Hospital, where I spent two weeks being treated. My time there gave me first-hand experience of Ulrich's research (1984) on the view from hospital beds. He demonstrated that beds with a view of natural environments triggered positive emotional reactions because observing nature was once important for human survival. My bed on the ward was next to a huge wall of windows which looked out to the hills beyond Inverness. I struggled hugely with being 'cooped up', missing the feeling of the elements on my face and was desperate to breathe fresh air. That view from the window kept me sane for two weeks; it was my one link to the natural world. All I wanted to do was get well enough to get out there again. Ulrich's research proved that people who had a natural view had a speedier post-operative discharge than those who had the view of a brick wall. I'd have to agree; there was one day where I was moved to a different ward which had a view of a brick wall and it was my bleakest day in hospital. When I was discharged my ankle had been pinned and plated back together but I wasn't going to be working in the outdoors anytime soon, so I figured that I had best find a job that was less physically demanding.

Corporate Life

My corporate career began at Mars Inc in 2000. To this day I'm still not sure how I got through the interview. I had no idea what all the TLAs (three-letter acronyms) were, no appreciation for the size and prestige of the organisation and no idea about business. I remember thinking, '*I'm not sure what all the fuss is about; it's just selling Mars bars, how hard can it be?*' However, they must have seen something in me as I spent 16 years working for this amazing global business. Eight of those years were in commercial roles before moving into people development. I worked with many people and all levels, teams and individuals. I had the privilege of Mars investing in my development as I grew in this field and I cannot thank Mars enough for all they gave me. Those latter eight years were a real opportunity to hone my executive coaching and team development skills, bringing together my outdoor development background, my corporate understanding and, towards the end, the experience from my Executive Coaching MSc. My action research dissertation was on 'How are we in nature and how does it affect the quality of our coaching conversations?' I am so grateful for all the experience I gained and for the invaluable feedback I got along the way.

Ocean Racing

In 2011/12, I took a sabbatical from Mars to race a sailing yacht through the world's largest oceans in the Clipper Round the World Yacht Race. It was indeed an experience of a lifetime: wildlife, vast oceans, the power of nature and being tested to my limits. As well as an extreme sailing adventure, the race was a personal development journey. I learnt about my limits, leadership in life-and-death situations, self-leadership, the importance of aligned values and the impact of remote organisational culture and politics on the front line. A highly valuable lesson, in the context of the coaching outdoors practice that this book is about, is that when your full capacity is taken up with survival, there is nothing left for self-awareness, introspection, reflection and learning, or certainly not until all is calm; it cannot be accessed in the moment. Nor can it for a while afterwards, due to exhaustion and relief initially delaying any processing. A valuable insight for someone who used to give less consideration to her client's comfort and capability than she should have! Should you have an interest in reading my blog from the race, you'll find it here: www.robertsroundtheworld.co.uk

Mother Nature

My purpose in life has now expanded to include, very specifically, my daughter Torrin: to give her the best opportunity to be happy and healthy in life. A critical foundation of this is for her to have a strong conscious bond with the natural world (I'd argue that the bond is there for us all as we are all inextricably part of the natural system, but for most of us the awareness has become mute). You'll find us following the annual cycle of the local swans on the canal (bringing up two signets as I write). Torrin loves feeding and chatting to them and experiencing each stage of their life cycle: the anticipation of hatching, fear of death from fox or otter, peeping out from behind a parent's wings, celebrating them growing and their feathers turning from brown to white. In the garden we listen to birds (I'd love to say that we identify them by sound but I'm clueless), plant vegetables (I end up doing the maintenance until they are ready to pick!), get excited when the squirrel visits and compete on butterfly spotting. On holidays at the beach, I watch as Mother Nature engages my daughter in a search for seashells and sea glass to decorate her sandcastles and sand-maids. Mother Nature draws her to rock pools for sea anemones to kiss her fingers and challenges her to be quick enough to spot tiny fish before they dart behind rocks. We take barefoot beach cleaning walks and are always saddened by how much we find. I watch my daughter in awe of her ability to be fully present and connected to nature. Each engagement fully absorbs her wholeheartedly. It's a gift for both her and the planet. I wish we could all hold onto that gift; perhaps then we'd be doing a better job as a species than we currently are to protect our home.

My Work Today

Today you'll find me working with individuals, teams and groups, combining my business experience, coaching skills and passion for the outdoors through the businesses I run – Brave Conversations and Coaching Outdoors – and in my work as an associate of Ashridge Business School. Each of the elements is aligned to my purpose of 'supporting people to unlock their potential'. The work outlined below are my big pebbles creating ripples in the sea!

Brave Conversations (www.braveconversations.co.uk) supports business leaders, executive-level teams and managers to fulfil their potential. We coach, mentor, train and design bespoke interventions for employees' development. Each of our team has corporate experience and relevant qualifications in their specialist area. The strength of the organisation lies in the collaborative partnerships we have with our clients and our ability to understand what is needed to really create change. We have great clients and I'm incredibly proud of the high quality of work that we deliver.

I launched Coaching Outdoors (www.coachingoutdoors.com) in 2019 as a result of my passion and experience in what nature can offer for coaching and developmental conversations. I realised that there was an opportunity for supporting other coaches and line managers to incorporate this powerful way of working in their practice and that there was very little available to help people step into this work. The mission of the organisation is to make coaching outdoors as accessible as possible to as many people as possible for the benefit of the coach, coachee, organisation and planet through providing a stimulating experience for personal and professional growth and wellbeing. I am incredibly proud to offer two European Coaching & Mentoring Council (EMCC) award-winning development programmes designed to support coaches and line managers taking their coaching conversations outdoors. Not only do the programmes share research and provide practical information, they also offer a personal development and wellbeing journey for the participants along the way. We also run a personal development retreat in the wilderness of Scotland and offer a variety of other resources. I share more detail about CoachingOutdoors.com in the appendices.

Both my companies and being a mother keep me pretty busy and doing what I love. When I get the chance, I like nothing more than spending time walking on long empty beaches, falling off a surfboard or cycling the quiet country roads around where I live. Occasionally, I'm lucky enough to get up to Scotland and spend time in the hills, which feeds my soul.

What You Will Find in This Book

MANY PROFESSIONS, INCLUDING architects, musicians, poets, engineers, artists, designers and more, draw inspiration from nature, bringing natural collaboration into their work: patterns, geometry, colour, sounds, smells and processes. Yet coaching, in the main, until very recently has not seen the opportunity to collaborate with nature.

Since 2020, Peter Hawkins has been inviting coaches to walk with a lightly held question: *'What can the wider ecology teach me about how to coach?'* He suggests that after a while the question may change to: *'How can I help you, the wider ecology, do most of the coaching?'* and *'What do you need me to do differently in order that you have the space to coach?'*

I'm filled with a sense of potential, that the coaching profession is becoming aware of the possibilities and systemic benefits to be gained from inviting nature into the coaching relationship.

For those coaches, line managers and leaders who want to take part in that journey, this essential guide is designed to equip you with all you need to know. I'm unaware of any other book in this specific field and am hopeful that this is the first of many because this niche is incredibly rewarding for coach, coachee, organisation and the planet.

Inside you will find research, inspirational real-life stories from coaches and their coachees, along with ideas, templates and tools. There are also some powerful and engaging activities for you throughout and suggestions for exercises and questions you can use with clients. It can be referred to again and again in preparation for coaching sessions or for some CPD. You will find it accessible, practical and personally developmental. Where clients' and coaches' names are shared, it is with their full permission. Others have been anonymised but their stories, feedback or ideas are still included for the rich value that they add for the reader.

A colleague of mine once said about our work: '*We stand on the shoulders of giants.*' It's a phrase that has resonated with me since. Without those '*giants*' this book would not be possible. Many chapters are enriched by knowledge and insight from others. I'd like to acknowledge the work of those who have preceded me and those who are running alongside; without them, this book would offer less and I would not have developed so far.

'*If there's a straight line in nature, a human drew it*' (author unknown). Interestingly I have found that mirrored in this book. I quite like things to be linear – easy to follow – and try as I might I've been unable to completely separate the elements of this essential guide into a linear process. It is much more of a web – one strand connected to multiple other strands. Much more like the matrix structure in many organisations. John Muir sums it up beautifully: '*When we try to pick out anything by itself, we find it hitched to everything else in the universe.*' So, you'll find that topics interconnect through different chapters and appear more than once. If I've done a good job, then when they reappear it will be with relevance and new insight, not repetition. So, for those of you who like everything neatly in one place, apologies for little gems popping up later on once you thought a topic was complete.

We begin, in Section I, by looking at exactly what coaching outdoors is and why it is growing so quickly in popularity. In Section II I invite you to consider our systemic connection to nature and our place in the universe, which leads nicely into the health and wellbeing benefits of being outside. And specifically, the neuroscience behind the benefits that walking outdoors brings to thinking and creativity. Some of these sections are heavier with academic research and data than later in the book. A valuable colleague of mine encouraged me to flag this to you so that you are prepared for a journey from the more academic to growing colour, nature and stories as you read on.

Then, we take a look at why, in today's fast-moving world, receiving coaching outdoors can benefit not just coachees but coaches, organisations and the planet. This is done through research, stories and insights from some skilled and inspiring coaching practitioners and a variety of organisations. I have also had the privilege of talking to clients who have received coaching outdoors and been prepared to share their story.

In Section III we then dive into getting you fully equipped for that first coaching session outdoors, addressing the common questions of 'What to wear?', 'Where to go?', 'What to do if it rains?' and 'How to make it safe?' I share some of my own experiences and learning, things that worked and things that didn't! All the foundations you need to get going.

Importantly, in Section IV, there's an opportunity for you to consider your connection with nature and how to congruently add coaching outdoors into your practice and conversations. There's also a provocation for you around your own practice in nature and how you embrace all that being outside can offer you for your development.

Inside you'll find case studies and practices to help you develop your outdoor coaching practice further; from taking your usual style of coaching conversation outside to partnering with nature as a co-facilitator in the coaching relationship. In Section V we explore metaphor, mirroring and seasons (my favourite).

In Section VI I also cover working outdoors with groups and teams and how to bring nature into our coaching conversations in a world where remote coaching is rapidly increasing. Lastly, in Section VII, I share my view on the future of coaching and coaching outdoors. In the appendices you will find a sample risk assessment form and other helpful resources.

Throughout, I use the words *client* and *coachee* interchangeably. For those coaches reading this, both words will resonate with you. For line managers and others who practise coaching the word *coachee* will be most relevant. I notice that I use both words in relation to my work and the book is a reflection of that.

Ultimately, I believe coaching outdoors provides a stimulating experience for personal and professional growth and wellbeing. My purpose is to help unlock that for as many people as possible and possibly achieve the even higher purpose of care for the environment, which begins with making a connection to nature at a personal level and then letting ownership for protecting the planet evolve from there.

Just as we are constantly learning about our planet and making new discoveries all the time, the same will be true in this work. There will always be more to learn and explore. But for now, dive in and let this book with its research, stories and resources inspire you to coach outdoors and develop your own relationship with nature along the way. Even better if you have the opportunity to read it in a natural setting!

Section I

Setting the Scene

What is Coaching?

I'M GUESSING THAT many reading this will be familiar with coaching and its standard definitions. I will offer a brief overview so that, if it is new to you, you have the background on it, and for others, it will give you a sense of my orientation to coaching. Here are some definitions:

'Coaching is unlocking a person's potential to maximise their own performance. It is helping them to learn rather than teaching them' (Whitmore, 2002, p.8).

'A process that enables learning and development to occur and thus performance to improve' (Parsloe, 1999, p.8).

'Coaching is a thought-provoking and creative partnership that inspires clients to maximize their personal and professional potential, often unlocking previously untapped sources of imagination, productivity and leadership' (International Coaching Federation website, 2022).

There are many types of coaching, including life coaching, sports coaching and mentoring. In this book, the focus is on executive coaching, sometimes called business or professional coaching. That is not to say that personal circumstances are never spoken about; of course they are: the professional who turns up for work every day brings with them all of their circumstances, history and experience. It would be naive to ignore all the things that make us who we are and shape how we approach situations. Executive coaching is usually focused on supporting professionals to be successful in their working world. I believe that coaches should also acknowledge that while their client may be the CEO, they are also a mother, daughter, sister, friend, athlete and indeed may even have a sense of humour! Our role is to coach the whole person, not just the job title.

Coaching first gained prominence in around the 18th century. However, the role of the coach has changed dramatically over the years – from being part of many different forms such as spiritual guru, philosopher, natural healer, counsellor and mentor to the professional coaching we recognise today. Coaching is now the second-biggest growing industry globally (ICF, 2020), with team and executive coaching in particular on the rise as organisations invest in developing their people to support them in our increasingly complex and demanding world.

In organisations, coaching has taken a more dominant role as a means of developing leadership, increasingly required as a key competitive advantage in today's world. Not only are senior leaders retaining coaching services, but those responsible for the management and performance of others are learning coaching skills in order to support the development and performance of their direct reports and teams. In many organisations, coaching cultures are developing to unlock the abilities of people often restricted by more traditional methods and styles of management.

A 2016 ICF survey highlighted that all those using coaching either on a personal basis or within the workplace aspired, as a key driver, to improve both individual and business performance. Coachees often comment on the value that coaching has had for them in helping them to achieve their goals and in supporting a new outlook on life which has come from a range of learnings and insights. They are more certain, motivated and true to themselves and able to achieve their full potential through greater self-esteem and confidence. With the achievement of the coachee's own potential comes the achievement of greater success to those around them.

I wrote above about coaching 'the whole person'. Of the various psychological theories, my coaching style is most closely aligned to Rogers's person-centred (1961) approach, which John Whitmore explains as follows: '[people] are more like an acorn, which contains within it all the potential to be a magnificent oak tree' (2002, p.9). I believe that my role as coach is to explore with my clients how to unlock *their* potential, not the potential they have for the role that they do!

Finally, it is important to acknowledge the evolution of coaching from the GROW model, where the coach follows a process, to relational coaching, which Professor Eric de Haan, director of coaching at Ashridge Hult Business School, describes in comparison to more traditional methods: 'Those approaches are full of ways to "handle" the client, and offer often explicit preferences for specific interventions or procedures. Relational coaching says that none of that matters very much' (de Haan, 2008, p.viii). He goes on to say: 'The relational approach… means having the courage to put the coachee truly at the centre of the coaching, rising above all those models and philosophies *for the coach*' (2008, p.ix; emphasis in original). I love that relational coaching puts the client at the centre and allows us to 'throw the process out the window'. It excites me to see what emerges in a coaching session, what the client feels will be of most use to them, in both the topics covered and in the tools or processes used. To me, relational coaching feels filled with freedom just as being outdoors does.

What is Coaching Outdoors?

In every walk with nature one receives far more than he seeks.

John Muir, 1914

Here I explore coaching outdoors in its simplest form to its richest and set it in context with other outdoor practices. I also give a view on what coaching outdoors is not.

Coaching draws significantly from humanistic and positive psychology and from some of the more shorter-term therapy models, including cognitive behavioural therapy and solution-focused therapy. Just as with humanistic and transpersonal psychotherapists, the underlying belief held by coaches is that you are already whole, and you already have everything you need to succeed. It's the coach's job to ask you the right questions and guide you towards your own inner resources.

Coaching outdoors is all of the above taken outside. Ideally on a walk together but also possibly on the phone. Or, if working virtually, bringing nature into the conversation and taking time between sessions to spend outdoors in service of the coaching journey. Dependent on the skill and experience of the coach, nature is either a passive or an active participant; I talk more about this later in the chapter.

In its most accessible form, coaching outdoors is holding a coaching session in the grounds outside the office building. I used to work for Mars Inc in the Slough office and would often have coaching conversations sitting on a wall in the sunshine in the car park or on a bench in the roof garden. If you are lucky enough to be working with someone who has an office near a park or in the countryside, then coaching outdoors could be taking a stroll through the park or meandering through the local woodlands or track along the side of the field. Although I have mentioned strolling and meandering, you may be sitting on a log or a bench or a mixture of both. The key is that you are outside and not within the four walls of the office or in the local Hilton!

A richer coaching intervention involves more than simply taking the same practice from an indoor to an outdoor space. The location is likely to be less urban, setting the scene for the more-than-human world to actively partic-ipate, offering more than an attractive backdrop. Coaches who work in this way recognise that nature has its own agency and role to play in coaching. I often use Rutland Water in the middle of England, a rural location with open views over the water, woodland paths and plenty of wildlife, yet is 15 minutes from a major road. Here, nature can support our conversation, sometimes without my mention of it, though often the clients do: '*Oh wow, the view is stunning*' or '*This is nice*'. I have never had anyone say that to me in an office meeting room. So, already we are off to a positive start! Or I can invite nature into the conversation, expanding the relationship and opening the door to additional dimensions, unlocking things which would unlikely have been reached without nature's active presence. For example, offering a client a moment of reflection while leaning on a gate at a clearing in the woods looking out over the water at small sailing boats, while I walk on a short way. Giving them the space to reflect on the conversation so far. Could you imagine doing this while sitting across a desk from someone? Even if you were to 'pop out to get the drinks', the coachee has not been left in an environment which positively supports meaningful reflection.

Another example of working collaboratively with nature comes from when I was working with a team in Devon; I invited them each to take a walk for 10 minutes and to pick up something they were drawn to and to bring it back.

We sat in a clearing in the woods while they shared what they had collected, why they were drawn to it and in what way they felt it was relevant to them. The quality of the conversation was far deeper, richer and more honest than we could have achieved had I asked them to do the same in a meeting room. Nature is a living, sensual place that evokes all the senses and communication channels: physical, emotional, imaginative and spiritual (Abram, 1996; Roszak, 2001). Working with nature as a partner in coaching can be transformational for coach and client.

In describing outdoor development experiences, Beringer and Martin (2003) note that the power of the experience may not lie solely with the coach alone: 'Rather, what may be equally critical if not more so, in bringing about change for the better may be due to "nature" – being in interaction with the natural worlds' (p.33). You'll find a whole chapter dedicated to this in the *Nature as Co-Facilitator* element of the book.

Nature-Based Interventions

In a world of ever-increasing noise, haste, technology and virtual worlds, it's no surprise that the following are all growing (rekindled in some cases!) fields: Wilderness Therapy, Adventure Therapy, Ecotherapy, Walking Therapy, Nature Therapy, Ecological Transational Analysis, Blue/Green Coaching, Shinrin-Yoku/Forest Bathing and Questing. Let's take a look at each in turn and place coaching outdoors in context with them.

Wilderness Therapy is the use of wild remote areas that are far removed from the pressures and immediate issues of today's society. It provides a secure, non-critical and supportive environment for self-discovery. In the main, wilderness therapy is geared towards teens and young adults who are suffering from behavioural, mental health or substance abuse concerns. It removes them from their home environment, where they are most at risk from these challenges, for an extended period of time (often 21 or so days). David Strayer, a cognitive neuroscientist, has concluded in his research that 'an immersion in nature of more than 3 days allows the prefrontal cortex, the brain's command centre, to dial down and rest, like an overused muscle' (Atchley et al., 2012, p.2). As a result, we become more creative and present. In wilderness therapy, this presence and creativity allow participants to think beyond the behavioural patterns they have become conditioned to. The origins of wilderness therapy have roots in the work of the German educator

Kurt Hahn, who founded the 'Outward Bound' organisation; as a result, the therapy often involves adventurous activities that take participants to the edge of their comfort zone in terms of endurance and adaptability.

Adventure Therapy is experiential using activities involving risk and physical and emotional challenges. The work is often done in groups and can be typified by the work of Kurt Hahn's 'Outward Bound' organisation founded in 1961. Adventure therapy theory draws from a mixture of learning and psychological theories. The ideas and thinking of Alfred Adler, Albert Ellis, Milton Erickson, William Glasser, Carl Jung, Abraham Maslow, Jean Piaget, Carl Rogers, B. F. Skinner, Fritz Perls and Viktor Frankl all appear to have contributed to the thinking in adventure therapy.

Ecotherapy is a form of psychotherapy rooted in the idea of Edward Wilson's Biophilia hypothesis: people's bond between themselves and other ecosystems. The specific features of ecotherapy include interaction with wild or semi-natural areas of nature and that nature is the primary therapeutic source for mental health and psychological and emotional wellbeing. The concept of ecotherapy is very ancient. Thousands of years ago, Shamans saw nature as being integral to health, healing and wellbeing.

Walking Therapy is a lighter touch than ecotherapy. Still outdoors but nature is not always a conscious active participant for either therapist or coach. Possible in urban areas.

Nature Therapy is an 'experiential approach based on the integration of elements from art and drama therapy, Gestalt, narrative, eco-psychology, transpersonal psychology, adventure therapy, shamanism and body-mind practices' (Berger & McLeod, 2006, p.87). The approach was developed by Ronen Berger. Berger encourages the client to choose a therapy space in nature, encouraging them to 'build a home' for their sessions, a safe and sacred space. In so doing, this gives them choice and control. This outdoor therapy room changes with the seasons and is alive compared to the sterile therapy room indoors. Working with nature empowers the client to take shared responsibility for the therapeutic process. Berger also works with rituals, stating that this is one of the central principles of nature therapy.

Ecological Transactional Analysis (Eco-TA) is a very recent emergent movement within transactional analysis. The first programme ran in January 2020. It is based on the theory that the human experience is one component in a wider system of connections. Eco-TA is 'the practice of transactional analysis in alliance with Earth' (Barrow & Marshall, 2020, p.4).

Blue/Green Coaching is another title for coaching outdoors, highlighting that the session will be carried out in an environment where water is present (blue) or trees, fields, grass and plants (green).

Lastly, we have Questing and Shinrin-Yoku/Forest Bathing. These mention neither coaching nor therapy and may not involve conversations in the traditional sense!

Shinrin-Yoku is the Japanese form of forest bathing which began in the 1980s. It is literally the practice of taking a bath in the forest, engaging all five senses to connect with the environment and clear the mind through being mindful. Dr Qing Li, the author of *Shinrin-Yoku: The Art and Science of Forest Bathing*, believes that Shinrin-Yoku is a preventative medicine, not a treatment. A typical session would see you walking slowly through a wood, savouring the sounds, smells and sights of nature and letting the forest in. Letting your body be your guide, being led by smell, colours and patterns, the feeling of leaves, ferns and bark, and somatic resonance. The session might end with breathing deeply while lying down under trees and looking up through the branches. 'It doesn't matter if you don't get anywhere. You are not going anywhere,' says Li (2018, p.12). In a nutshell, it's about engaging mindfully with the forest; slowing down mentally and physically, not strolling through on a dog walk or on the phone.

Questing interventions are more spiritual and less 'mainstream' than anything already covered. They have their roots in tribal rites of passage.

A **Medicine Walk** is a ritual of solo wandering in nature. A fasting day out in nature from sunrise to sunset, it often takes place as preparation for a Vision Quest. It begins the journey of being open to the 'other-than-human' realm. The premise is to go out into nature and see 'what comes'. It involves '[b]eing open to an innate systemic intelligence outdoors, so whatever we end up "thinking" is where we need to be' (Macmillan, pers. comm.). While the process has 'walk' in the title, a typical medicine walk would be a mix of walking, sitting, meditating, even sleeping.

A **Vision Quest** is a rite of passage in some Native American cultures. It is mainly undertaken by young males entering adulthood. The process includes a complete fast for four days and nights, alone at a sacred site in nature. The objective is to help them find their purpose in life, their role in the community and how they may best serve their people. The Western objective is usually for personal growth, becoming more aware and having a deeper connection. Participants are often, but not always, drawn to questing during times of change or desiring change. It creates time for contemplation and for reconnecting with one's self and the natural world, bringing clarity through communing with nature. The format is usually a solo period of three or four days and nights in nature, bracketed by time with experts who guide the process – taking care of you, managing safety, your health, teaching and leading ceremonies and the integration of your experience into your 'normal' life. An intriguing summary would be: 'a sacred adventure of discovery with visible and invisible worlds'.

Perhaps the most obvious difference in the fields listed above is that most are titled either coaching or therapy. So that's a good place to start. Some would say that coaches work with healthy clients and are future focused, while therapists work with 'issues' and focus on the past, but we know that's not true. Here's my offering for the differences:

Psychotherapy is often described as a journey of the soul; a deep exploration of your inner and outer world. For whatever reason, you may be suffering and you may have lost contact with your true self; through the therapeutic relationship with your therapist, psychotherapy seeks to restore and renew this connection. The primary purpose of therapy is to build a healthy relationship with your 'self', others and the world at large. The primary purpose of coaching is to support clients in reaching their potential.

The most obvious difference between coaching and therapy is that coaches are not trained to diagnose or work with mental health concerns such as anxiety, depression, past trauma, and any other underlying issues. Most coaching requires a baseline level of good health to be effective and coaches are advised to refer on clients who they feel unequipped to support.

Psychotherapy and coaching can both offer life-changing experiences and often the dividing line between the two can be a little grey!

Key to all these practices is the concept of nature as a partner in the relationship; most often as an active partner, a kind of co-facilitator. Then there is the sliding scale of where the therapist or coach places themselves in relation to nature. You can see this in the 'Nature as co-facilitator dynamic' figure.

The therapist [/coach] may take a central position, working directly with the client and relating to nature as a backdrop or tool provider. The therapist [/coach] may also take a quieter role, remaining in the background, allowing the client to work directly with nature while the therapist [/coach] acts as a witness, container, and mediator.

(Berger & McLeod, 2006, p.83)

NATURE AS CO-FACILITATOR DYNAMIC

Taking the indoor conversation outside

Stepping back and allowing nature to be the coach

Lesley Roberts 2020

We will explore this in more depth in the 'Nature as a Co-Facilitator' section of the book.

So that brings us back to the outdoors. Being outside is common to all, as is the belief that being outdoors is beneficial. And, in most fields where there is a conversation (perhaps sometimes an activity) over a typical session of 60–90 minutes, the locations will be the same: urban parks, National Trust grounds, woods, canals, reservoirs. Where the sessions are longer, a full day to a number of days, it is likely in all cases that the locations become a little wilder: moors, national parks, mountains. It's the activities and conversations that differ.

So, where does that leave us? There are a variety of 'ways of working' with the natural world. Having clarity on where our practice sits, what we do and why enables us to manage our clients' expectations and ensure their psychological safety.

Having a background in outdoor education, wilderness therapy and adventurous activities, I'm often asked about coaching, leadership development or high-performance teamwork in adventurous or extreme environments. These requests have prompted me to reflect on what my beliefs are around this. What coaching outdoors is not, in my opinion, although others may disagree, is crossing the Channel on a sailing yacht, climbing Ben Nevis or abseiling down the Empire State Building (these would all come under Adventure Therapy). I hold a belief that, as a general rule, both coach and coachee need to be comfortable in the environment so that all of their available capacity for learning, reflection and awareness can be engaged in the coaching experience, not taken up with whether or not they are going to be seasick, have a painful blister or lose their fingers in some daunting equipment. I look at this in more detail further on in the book.

Why is Coaching Outdoors Growing?

One of the first conditions of happiness is that the link between Man and Nature shall not be broken.

Leo Tolstoy, 1910

IN THIS CHAPTER, we take a look at what is happening in the world today; the challenges and threats everyone is facing. I share the high demands that leaders are under and offer insight into the experience of what it's like in today's society. Coaching outdoors can counter some of the impact of those demands and pressures and offer perspective. We also look at why Covid-19 has accelerated people's adoption of coaching outside and the impact that the growing awareness of the climate crisis has had on the growth of coaching outdoors.

We all know the phrase 'strike while the iron is hot'. Well, the iron is red hot for coaching outdoors. Let's take a look at why, starting with a conversation I had in early 2019:

> I was talking about coaching outdoors to an ex-Mars colleague. She mentioned that the majority of people in her sector of the business now go out for a walk at least once a day. We reflected on how it used to be that those who were already converts to the outdoors, or, the 'healthy bunch', used to go out, but now it is almost everyone. She said the management team all have their development conversations outside walking and that 50% of line

managers' one-to-one conversations were outside, whether that be in person or over the phone.

I asked what had made the difference; she replied: '*The general well-being agenda that the business has been following for a number of years and crucially the GM going outdoors for all his one-to-one conversations.*'

The World Today

That was three years ago; today (mid-2022), the wellbeing agenda is even more critical to organisations and individuals. Our world today is facing major economic, environmental, political and technological change. The speed of developments in these areas affects all of our lives. Globally we see some key trends:

- Climate change and increasing scarcity and ethics of resources
- An increasing global population, and with it rapid urbanisation
- The uncertainty and fear of further global pandemics
- Emergence of the digital era
- Exponential rate of change in the development of technologies
- Increased individual empowerment and therefore expectations
- Greater cultural and generational diversity in the workplace than ever before
- Continued political instability

Demands on Leaders Today

Today, those business leaders in Mars, and of course all other organisations who make up a large proportion of our coaching clients, will be facing demands to:

- Be an adept conceptual and strategic thinker
- Be able to create an engaging and trusting culture
- Have deep integrity and be able to be honest, humble and vulnerable
- Lead collaboratively and not necessarily from the top
- Know yourself and your purpose, be authentic
- Have exceptional EQ, not just IQ
- Be able to deal with ambiguity and be agile
- Guide organisations through the ever-increasing crisis they face

- Lead in a volatile, uncertain, complex and ambiguous (VUCA) world

As a result, we know that leaders are finding it increasingly difficult to balance work and life, being time poor and not always cash rich! They feel overwhelmed with what is expected of them, the size of their role and the amount of data and information they are expected to have a handle on. They are experiencing the pressure of deciding which are the critical focus areas when so much information is available, and the game is always changing. They need to know, in the ever-growing matrixed organisation, how to get things done with conflicting agendas and unclear reporting lines. And just as leaders think that they have achieved something, it's all change – change is the only constant and it is becoming more rapid! It is no wonder that employees are at risk of burnout and that organisations are focusing on development, resilience and wellbeing to help their staff survive. Coaching outdoors is a solution to much of this.

Society Today

More broadly in society, there is a need to improve mood and mental health in general. Over the past century, people have been increasingly concentrated in urban areas. In many instances, they spend longer in artificial environments using electronic devices and being sedentary. As technology has developed, we have moved away from nature and, it feels, from human connection. We've shifted from mystical, religious and tribal life in reciprocation with nature to an individualistic, capitalist urban life. These conditions have a negative effect on our general wellbeing. Depression and anxiety are problems that are increasing significantly in the UK, as shown by the following statistics from Aquafolium (no date):

- 2.6% (19,700) of the population experience depression and 4.7% (35,600) have anxiety problems; as many as 9.7% (73,500) suffer mixed depression and anxiety, making it the most prevalent mental health problem in the population as a whole.
- About 1.2% (9,100) of the population experience panic disorders.
- Around 1.9% of adults (12,000) experience a phobia of some description, and women are twice as likely to be affected by this problem as men.

- Post-traumatic stress disorder (PTSD) affects 2.6% of men (9,600) and 3.3% of women (12,800).
- Obsessive compulsive disorder (OCD) affects around 2–3% (15,200–22,700) of the population.
- Generalised anxiety disorder affects between 2% and 5% of the population (15,200–37,900), yet accounts for as much as 30% of the mental health problems seen by GPs.

The number of antidepressants given to patients in England doubled between 2005 and 2015, official figures show (Meikle, 2016). In 2015 there were 61 million such drugs prescribed and dispensed outside of hospitals. They are used to treat clinical depression, as well as other conditions such as generalised anxiety disorder, obsessive compulsive disorder and panic attacks. The total was 31.6 million more than in 2005 and up 3.9 million, or 6.8%, on 2014, according to a report from the Health and Social Care Information Centre (HSCIC) referred to in an article in the *Guardian*. The article reports that: 'The net cost of ingredients of antidepressants, before taking account of any money reclaimed by the NHS, was nearly £285m last year' (Meikle, 2016).

While the business world pressures may only affect those employed in corporate organisations, the societal trends affect all of us – that is, every person that we coach! In the coming pages, I'll share the valuable wellbeing benefits of coaching outdoors.

Covid-19 Impact

We also know that everyone will have had an experience of the Covid-19 pandemic and been affected by it in some way.

Coronavirus has created a global challenge, yet it has also created huge opportunities. One of those opportunities has been our relationship with the natural world. In the UK, the governmental advice during Covid-19 lockdowns of daily exercise in the fresh air has gone a long way to increasing the nation's first-hand awareness of the physical and mental benefits of being outdoors. We were forced to break our routines and habits and create new ones, some of which began to enhance our time outdoors and our appreciation for nature as a place of safety and sanctuary. Covid-19 highlighted the importance of contact with green and blue spaces for fostering our ability to cope with the stress and threat of the virus, and the physical restrictions imposed in response to it. The natural world took on a new role for many people as an alternative place for physical activity and social interaction. I know I am not going to be alone in having met up with friends in gardens, bundled up, in the depths of winter. We even celebrated Christmas Eve with our neighbours, one at a time, as we stood on driveways and ate socially distanced mince pies and mulled wine. The outdoors became a 'safe' space for meeting people. And of course, this thread spanned into the world of coaching. Suddenly, any perceived barriers to coaching outdoors fell away and it became the 'safe' and 'healthy' option for both coach and coachee. Almost overnight, coaching outdoors became a 'go to' for many.

Climate Crisis

The ever-increasing climate crisis has been the single biggest factor in previously solely indoor coaches (the vast majority of the coaching population) offering their clients the opportunity to connect with nature and get outside. Why? Well, the coaching industry has begun to provoke coaches on what their response is to the climate crisis. The desire to work outside, which we shared 50:50 with our clients through Covid-19, has certainly moved to a pull from coaches to include nature as part of the coaching experience. One of the strongest voices has been from Peter Hawkins, Professor of Leadership and Coaching at Henley Business School and thought leader and practitioner across a number of fields in coaching. He has been provoking coaches to move beyond the 'coach and coachee agenda' to 'being on life's agenda' (Hawkins, 2020). Hawkins believes that coaches have a role to play in the climate crisis facing the world and that in our contracting conversations with our coachees we should ask 'How are we going to attend to the more-than-human/ecological world in our coaching?' (Hawkins, 2020, slide 14). His provocation has been met with some resistance due to its leading nature – coaches using their 'power' (Bergen et al., 2006) to influence the client's agenda. However, what he has done is further pique coaches' interest in the outdoors. Especially as he describes, in some of his talks, the coaching retreats that he runs, where coaching in nature is part of the experience. Hawkins gets his attendees to walk through his woodland and '*let the nature in as a resource*'. He gives them a challenge – '*How do they use the trees, how do they use the birds?*', getting the environment to do the coaching, not just each other. In the process of all that he is driving at, he is shifting mindsets about coaching outdoors and the value that nature can offer to coaching.

Hawkins is also a leading participant in the newly formed Climate Coaching Alliance (CCA). Set up in November 2019 by Alison Whybrow, Eve Turner and Josie McLean, the CCA's aim, as noted on their website, is to 'influence the global professional coaching community to bring in the deep and difficult questions of climate and ecological emergency into coaching conversations'. So far, it seems that many executive coaches are aware of the CCA. Again, the effect has been for coaches to reach out and find ways to partner with nature, but as of yet I have still to see evidence of coaches, overtly and uninvited, discussing climate issues with their clients. In the section on 'The Benefits of Coaching Outdoors', I'll share my view on the coach's role with regard to the climate crisis.

Both coach and client are now more open to working outdoors than ever before in a bid to counter some of life's numerous challenges and feel the benefit of spending some time in nature. There has never been a better time to suggest that your coaching sessions take place outside; the door is most definitely open!

Section II

The Benefits of Coaching Outdoors

Our Systemic Connection with Nature

You didn't come into this world.
You came out of it, like a wave from the ocean.
You are not a stranger here.

Alan Watts, 1973

IN THIS CHAPTER, we explore the importance of Alan Watts's quote and its relevance to coaching outdoors. Being outdoors in nature is not about embracing something new. It is about reconnecting with something we already know. It's in our DNA. In a world that embraces noise, pace and technology:

> ... there is a counter-movement: one that recognises our essential quality as part of nature. This movement invites us to reclaim our place in the universe, to remind us that we are organic relational beings who influence, and are profoundly influenced by the natural world.
>
> (McGeeney, 2016, p.9)

One of the basic concepts of coaching outdoors is that nature provides a therapeutic setting. Nature is a live dynamic environment that is not under the control or ownership of either the coach or the client. It is an open independent space, which has existed long before their arrival and will remain long after they depart. Nature reminds us that the world has not been made by humans. 'We have evolved amidst a complex web of nature' (Kellert & Wilson, 1995, p.65). We are systemically connected to nature. Many of us exist for most of the time in a world which is humanly arranged, themed and controlled. As technology has developed, we have moved away from nature; our devices have taken us from a life based around relationships with each other and the natural world to a more individualistic, urban norm. We have forgotten that not everything is controlled by the flick of a switch, pressing a button or talking to 'Alexa'. We've forgotten that we are a part of something bigger, wilder and more powerful than ourselves. Nature has her own rhythm, one much more connected to our DNA than a laptop ever will be. Nature poses profound questions about our focus, intent and contribution. Most importantly, nature provides a sense of wonder, an experience of beauty, greatness and strength beyond anything we could create.

> Whether it is the dark swirls which water makes beneath a plate of ice, or the feel of the soft pelts of moss which form on the lee side of boulders and trees... A snowflake a millionth of an ounce in weight falling on to one's outstretched palm... To hear how a hillside comes alive with moving water after a rain shower.
>
> (Macfarlane, 2008, p.275)

It is no great surprise that our screensavers, wallpaper, pictures and paintings are not of computers, office furniture or our colleagues but of nature, animals or our family! 'We are nature, it's not us and other, we are in relationship with it' (Allen, 2020, p.19).

While in our office or at a laptop, we are very much a part of an organisational system; we are experiencing it very vividly. Moving outside not only brings in physical movement but nature and perspective as we connect again to the ultimate system of the universe. Then, we see a beautiful simplicity, the other side of all this complexity and stress in today's world. Whenever we walk outside, we are sub-consciously connecting to the footsteps of those that have gone before us, be that someone on the same path an hour previously or 10,000 years ago! One of the participants from the 'Getting Started Coaching Outdoors' programme I run captured this beautifully when she wrote: '*It's funny isn't it how the outdoors takes us back to a time before we existed, when our ancestors lived their lives outside and it grounds us!*' – Lesley-Anne Cantwell, July 2020.

Evolution

For 99% of our time on Earth we lived as hunter-gatherers. No cities, no internet. Our ancestors only survived because they had an intimate connection to nature. For over 2.2 million years, our ancestors (in the genus *Homo*) etched out an existence within natural environments. To survive necessitated finding sustenance and shelter, and avoiding predators. These experiences have shaped many aspects of our modern brain functions. They continue to influence emotion, motivation, learning and reasoning in subtle ways. In addition, since our ancestral experience was mostly an outdoor one, sleep- and mood-regulating circadian rhythms became coordinated by the cycles of natural light. Just imagine what a sedentary, centrally heated, IT focused, electrically lit life is doing for us today both physically and mentally. Not to mention that many of us have lost the deep nature connection our ancestors had – sense of direction, lighting and tending a fire, finding water, edible and medicinal plants, moving silently and making things with our hands.

And that's just our ancestors. The Earth has been here for 4.6 billion years. We are all related to the first cell on Earth. Every single plant and animal can trace its ancestry to that first cell, which means we are all related to each other. Our spine, nervous system, heart and gut are all descended from fish. In the womb we breathe with gills and have a tail!

Strozzi-Heckler talks in evolutionary terms about our 'intuitive knowing': 'Over 3 billion years of embodied knowledge of survival, adapting, social intelligence, co-ordinating, intuition and reciprocity live largely unused in us' (Strozzi-Heckler, 2014, p.36). This largely explains why, when coaching outdoors, sometimes a client will say '*It just came to me*' or '*I've got it*'.

Our Relationship with the Earth

In 1855 a letter was sent by Native American Chief Seattle of the Duwamish Tribe to Franklin Pierce, President of the United States, in response to an offer to purchase the Duwamish lands in the north-east of the US, currently Washington State. The letter (excerpts of which are reproduced below) offers a very different perspective on the capitalist world's desire to dominate the planet.

> The Great Chief in Washington sends word that he wishes to buy our land.

> How can you buy or sell the sky – the warmth of the land? The idea is strange to us. Yet we do not own the freshness of the air or the sparkle of the water. How can you buy them from us? We will decide in our time. Every part of this earth is sacred to my people. Every shining pine needle, every sandy shore, every mist in the dark woods, every clearing, and every humming insect is holy in the memory and experience of my people.

> We know that the white man does not understand our ways. One portion of land is the same to him as the next, for he is a stranger who comes in the night and takes from the land whatever he needs. The earth is not his brother, but his enemy, and when he has conquered it, he moves on. He leaves his father's graves and his children's birth-right is forgotten. The sight of your cities pains the eyes of the redman. But perhaps it is because the redman is a savage and does not understand.

> There is no quiet place in the white man's cities. No place to listen to the leaves of spring or the rustle of insect wings. But perhaps because I am a savage and do not understand – the clatter only seems to insult the ears. And what is there to life if a man cannot hear the lovely cry of the whippoorwill or the arguments of the frogs around a pond at night? The Indian prefers the soft sound of the wind itself

cleansed by a mid-day rain or scented by a pinõn pine: The air is precious to the redman. For all things share the same breath – the beasts, the trees, and the man. The white man does not seem to notice the air he breathes. Like a man dying for many days, he is numb to the stench.

If I decide to accept, I will make one condition. The white man must treat the beasts of this land as his brothers. I am a savage and I do not understand any other way. I have seen thousands of rotting buffaloes on the prairie left by the white man who shot them from a passing train. I am a savage and do not understand how the smoking iron horse can be more important than the buffalo that we kill only to stay alive. What is man without the beasts? If all the beasts were gone, men would die from great loneliness of spirit, for whatever happens to the beast also happens to the man.

All things are connected. Whatever befalls the earth befalls the sons of the earth.

(Chief of the Suamisu Tribe, 1854)

Nature is necessary for our physical and psychological wellbeing. Interacting with nature teaches us to live in relation with the other, not in domination over the other: We don't control the birds flying overhead, or the Moon rising, or the bear walking where it would like to walk. One of the overarching problems of the world today is that we see ourselves living in domination rather than in relation with other people and with the natural world. If only more people related in the way Jim Crumley does:

Whenever I am in the company of great trees… the image that slips effortlessly into mind is that of a parliament of sages, exchanging essential truths about the world and its ways; discussing and refashioning the laws of nature. Their wisdom is the product of centuries of stillness, of rootedness, of loyalty to a sense of place and to nature's guiding principles.

(Crumley, 2020)

Or as the poet Gary Snyder (1990) puts it, 'Nature is not a place to visit. It is home.'

Being outside in nature re-establishes our vital and fundamental connection with the Earth. We relax and become more aware of what our intuition is telling us without all the 'noise' that usually blocks it out. Direct contact with 'the grand vistas of time and space' (Macfarlane, 2008, p.41) offers the opportunity to reach new perspectives. As Marshall (2016) notes, '[t]he vitality in the outdoor space invites a dynamic resonance inside us that has the power to evoke and support all kinds of important experiences'. Such is the impact that being outdoors, connected to nature, away from offices and technology, can bring to the coaching experience.

Planet Benefits

Our planet, struggling to live under the conditions we have created,
desperately needs us to reconnect and take steps towards repair.

Ruth Allen, 2021, p.19

IN THE LAST chapter we explored humans being part of the great web of life, completely interconnected and descended from our planet. The following words were written by Albert Einstein in 1950 to a man who was distraught over the death of his young son from polio; they are a great opening for this chapter:

> A human being is a part of the whole called by us universe, a part limited in time and space. He experiences himself, his thoughts and feeling as something separated from the rest, a kind of optical delusion of his consciousness. This delusion is a kind of prison for us, restricting us to our personal desires and to affection for a few persons nearest to us. Our task must be to free ourselves from this prison by widening our circle of compassion to embrace all living creatures and the whole of nature in its beauty.

In this chapter, I share how coaching outdoors can play an important role in the sustainability crisis the world today faces. If we wish to survive (I say 'we' referring to the human species, as Mother Earth will continue to evolve in response to what we have done without us!), then we need to take responsibility for making survival choices that maintain an environment that our and other species of today can tolerate. Unlike Peter Hawkins and the Climate Coaching Alliance, I don't believe it is the coach's role to bring questions of climate and ecological emergency into the coaching conversation. However, I do believe that we protect and defend what we love. Therefore, beginning with ourselves, we need to build a relationship with the natural world and fall in love with it – do our own work first! (I address this in Section IV.) Then, there is the role we can play in creating an opportunity for others to find their connection with nature. A heart-led approach. The action required to save our planet will not come from a cerebral place because the sacrifices required are too great. It will come from an emotional place deep within, unstoppable, even with the pain of the sacrifices required. It will come from a place driven by love. We protect what we love and will suffer any pain to do so. In this chapter, I propose that there are ecological benefits of taking our coaching conversations outside, based on the premise that through spending time engaging with nature in our coaching conversations we develop a level of nature connectedness. Let's take a look at what nature connectedness is and why it matters.

Nature Connectedness

Nature connectedness is the strength of a person's relationship with nature. It is more than simply visiting and being in nature. This quote from Marshall is a good expanded explanation:

> I believe that 'minding our landscape' also has implications for us developing more reciprocal relationships with the natural world; for, as a connective practice, it inherently evokes care for the place. Overall, this amounts to what I would term a sustaining transaction, where both individual and environment are potentially nourished by the contact.
>
> (Marshall, 2016)

Mackay and Schmitt (2019) define nature connection as the sense of one's 'openness' with nature, demonstrating that nature connectedness is a route to both human and nature's wellbeing. Their recent systemic review showed a causal relationship between nature connectedness and pro-environmental behaviours (Mackay & Schmitt, 2019). It highlighted that those who are in relationship with nature are likely to use fewer resources and 'take positive actions to help wildlife'.

Here's an experience from a client of mine (Gavin Wray, sales executive) illustrating his experience of moving from being outdoors to being in connection with nature:

Despite being from Yorkshire and living in a fabulous rural area with amazing scenery, rivers and forests on my doorstep, I've taken this a little for granted. I've enjoyed the feeling of being outdoors for most of my life playing sports like rugby and football, running and cycling, but it's fair to say that the 'outdoor' element has always been secondary to the actual activity I was doing. When out running, my focus was often on pacing myself correctly, preparing for the big hill that was just around the next bend or checking my stopwatch to see how I was measuring up against my target time. The route I took was pre-planned, measured and functional. I rarely even looked up, though have always enjoyed the challenge of the ever-changing weather.

I really did need to change my mindset for these self-coaching, connection walks and wind things down several notches. The slower pace of walking meant I had time to look around. I became aware of so much. Rather than just hearing a background engine noise, I noticed which field that tractor was in and stopped to look at what the farmer was doing. The overhead power cables on the pylons I have run beneath for 20+ years on my regular run, actually *sizzle* when it's raining… never noticed that before!!! How quickly do things grow??? Three weeks ago, I walked down a narrow track to get to a field; this week I'd need a machete to get through!!!

It's all been about allowing myself time to slow down and look up. You just put your boots on and get out there. Brilliant. I've loved it.

Pathways to Nature Connectedness

The University of Derby has developed the 'Pathways to Nature Connectedness Framework' from a three-year programme of research. As Gavin shared, it's more than just being outside exposed to nature. Connectedness is increased through:

- Senses – sensory contact, e.g. touching petals, walking on grass, listening to birds.

- Emotion – having meaningful experiences involving emotions: happiness, wonder, joy, calmness.
- Beauty – appreciation for nature's beauty.
- Meaning – belonging, purpose, relating to natural cycles, celebrating the longest day, for example.
- Compassion – care for nature: feed the birds, plant flowers, beach cleans, bug hotels.

You will find all five of these incorporated in the exercises, stories and research throughout this book.

The Coach's Role

I view the coach's role in the environmental agenda as one where we can (re)connect people with nature for the multi-faceted benefits that it brings: wellbeing both for us and the planet, coaching outcomes and business benefits. Coaching outdoors, incorporating the pathways to nature connection, is the powerful and active way that you can influence positive environmental change beyond your personal commitments.

But first begin with yourself. Section IV of this book will support you in that.

In Summary

> It is not science but love that will bring us back to nature time and time again. Love that we feel instinctively in our bones at an ancestral level, love for what is being lost, love for ourselves and each other and the great wish to alleviate suffering, love for the wonder and precarious brilliance of being alive in the universe on a beautiful planet.
>
> (Allen, 2021, p.186)

The climate emergency and crisis of biodiversity loss show that the human–nature relationship is failing. People will be more supportive of the big changes needed for a sustainable future if they are more connected to nature and feel that nature matters to them. Being outdoors, in relationship with nature, can soften our collective tread on the Earth.

We protect what we love

Activity – Connect with Nature

As you sit reading this, pause for a few moments and notice nature around you:

- Take a breath.
- What can you see?
- Are there any natural smells?
- Can you touch anything of nature from where you are?
- What natural sounds can you hear?

As you experience these things consider:

- What is evoked by the everyday nature encountered in your life?
- What meaning does this have for you?
- What if it wasn't there?

We must cherish the natural world because we're a part of it and we depend on it.

Sir David Attenborough

Wellbeing Benefits

*I go to nature to be soothed and healed, and to have
my senses put in order.*

John Burroughs, 1921

IF I WAS writing this book five or six years ago, I would have considered this chapter pivotal in raising awareness of the many benefits of being out-doors. However, the world has moved on considerably due to Covid-19, and the overwhelming scientific evidence that nature is good for our mental and physical health and wellbeing has risen in awareness and acceptance. The following is from a 2021 World Health Organization report (p.3):

> The ongoing COVID-19 pandemic, with the related societal measures and socioeconomic implications also affects mental health (Probst, Budimir & Pieh, 2020; van der Velden et al., 2020)… the main impact is elevated rates of stress and anxiety. However, with the introduced measures, such as quarantine and isolation, elevated levels of loneliness, depression, harmful substance use, self-harm and suicidal behaviour can be expected (WHO, 2020a; 2021a), adding to the already substantial burden of mental disorders in the population. Many tools to mitigate feelings of anxiety or depression exist, which may help in coping with mental distress. Getting out into nature, where and when permitted, and keeping active is one of these tools. That makes the role of access to nature, to green and blue spaces, even more significant for mental health, as a refuge for people to relax and socially interact, while adhering to COVID-19 restrictions.

Many of us experienced the benefits of nature through the pandemic and while we may not know the research or the stats, we know first hand that being outside makes us feel better. So, rather than dive in too deeply (as this chapter could easily be a book in itself), I'll share a summary of the researched benefits of spending time in nature, explore the benefits of walking, which help to emphasise the value of coaching outdoors, and then summarise two relevant theories: Biophilia and Attention Restoration.

Summary of Research

The model below is a visual summary of the benefits of spending time outdoors. If you'd like to understand some research that supports it, read on. If you would just like the executive summary, then skip to the part on economic benefits.

THE POSITIVE EFFECTS OF NATURE

PHYSICAL WELL-BEING
Improves cardiac functions, reduces hypertension, balances hormonal regulation, improves respiratory functioning, enhances eyesight.

SOCIAL WELL-BEING
Effective interpersonal communication, stronger bonds, deeper emotional attachment, empathy, less conflict and aggression at home.

HUMAN-NATURE CONNECTION

PSYCHOLOGICAL WELL-BEING
Emotional regulation, increased attention, positive thinking, improved stress management, resilience, mood upliftment.

SPIRITUAL WELL-BEING
Deeper sense of self, more gratitude, self-enhancement, increased insight towards the positive and negative aspects of life.

PositivePsychology.com B.V. 2019

I feel stronger and more alive by just being outside.
HG, coaching client, 2016

A good place to begin is with the research from the University of Derby on uncovering the crucial role nature plays in our overall happiness and well-being (Cormack et al., 2016). The study revealed that feelings of happiness and wellbeing were positively correlated with natural activities such as gardening, animal feeding, bird watching and rural walking. In this study, Dr Miles Richardson (the face of the study) shared evidence of how proximity to nature improved mood, enhanced respiratory functioning, regulated hormonal malfunctions and impacted on thought structure. Just by being outdoors and using all our senses to appreciate nature, we can be more mindful of the present, gain emotional resilience and combat stress with more vitality. We become naturally resilient to anxiety, emotional ups and downs and stuck thinking, and therefore feel livelier and more energetic. '*It was an oasis for me in this time of pandemic pressure. It reconnected me to the outdoors. Nature powerfully supported me, as a leader, as a coach and importantly as a human*' – Amanda Nelson, HRD QinetiQ, 2020.

Researchers at the University of Essex found that, out of a group of people with depression, 90% felt a higher level of self-esteem after taking a walk through a country park, and almost three-quarters of the group felt less dispirited after the walk (Barton & Pretty, 2010). Berman et al. (2012) found similar. They discovered that people with mild to major depressive disorders showed significant improvements in mood from increased endorphins when exposed to nature. Not only that, they also felt more motivated and energised to recover and get back to normalcy. This research correlates strongly with people citing increased confidence and better emotional regulation from spending regular time in nature.

In Japan, there have been 30 years of research on the benefits of immersing yourself in the forest, involving mind, body and senses being present. Spending time in the forest also brings physiological benefits for the immune system, lower cortisol levels and blood pressure, and therefore reduced stress. It is also known that being in nature and gently moving can help with chronic pain and inflammation.

According to research for the Mental Health Foundation carried out during the Covid-19 pandemic, 45% of people in the UK cited visiting green spaces as helping them cope with stress. Being outdoors reduces stress by lowering the stress hormone cortisol (Gidlow et al., 2016).

> Being in the outdoors, walking down a tree-lined street, having views of nature from a residential care window or walking slowly through a meadow have all been shown to lower stress response in healthy people as well as those with problems.
>
> (McGeeney, 2016, p.100)

Our relationship with nature – how much we notice, think about and appreciate our natural surroundings – is a critical factor in supporting good mental health. When it comes to mental health benefits, nature can mean green or blue spaces, urban street trees, private gardens, verges, even indoor plants or window boxes. Even watching nature documentaries has been shown to be good for mental health.

A study at the University of Kansas found that spending more time outdoors and less time with our electronic devices can increase our problem-solving skills and improve creative abilities (Atchley et al., 2012). Being outdoors can also lead to better decision making and systemic longer-term thinking. There is anecdotal evidence for this in the chapters on coach and client benefits.

Prescribing Nature

Ancient healers have known for centuries what much of society today is only beginning to pay attention to.

> Healers within various medical systems, from Ayurveda... to Chinese medicine, have long advocated nature exposure as a form of medicine. Within these healing systems, elements of nature – mountains, trees, plants, and bodies of water within natural settings – are considered to be filled with an energy, a vital force that could be transferred to people.
>
> (Selhub & Logan, 2014, pp.10–11)

There is a momentum of change in delivering patient-led outcomes beyond the standard medical model. Spring-boarding from growing evidence that standard pharmacological prescriptions are not the only approach, 'medical doctors began to prescribe nature exposure as a means of reducing stress and improving mental outlook' (Selhub & Logan, 2014, p.12). For example, in 2018, GPs on the Shetland Islands began issuing 'nature prescriptions', which instruct patients with chronic conditions to take strolls on beaches and moors, with a list of bird and plant species to look out for as they wander.

Evidence published by Sport England (2015) and Natural England (2022) reinforces the model presented at the beginning of the chapter, showing that activity in green environments leads to a 33% improvement in physical health outcomes, 80% reduction in social isolation and an overall increase in personal wellbeing. GPs now prescribe Green Gym sessions run by a group called The Conservation Volunteers (TCV). These sessions provide people with an opportunity to connect with nature and their community and co-create high-quality and sustainable green spaces. Hall notes that shared 'experiences in natural spaces lead to increased self-esteem, an increased internal locus of control' (2015, p.12). In urban centres like London, the number of green gyms has increased by 500% since 2011.

A final example of the movement in prescribing nature comes from the UK's Mental Health Foundation. In 2021, from all the wellbeing interventions available, the organisation focused on spending time in nature for Mental Health Awareness Week. Mark Rowland, Chief Executive of the Mental Health Foundation, invited us to 'open ourselves up and interact with nature'.

Benefits of Walking

We have looked in general at studies on the benefits of being outdoors and connected to nature. We're now going to explore deeper into walking outdoors because the act of walking is something rarely achieved coaching inside and is often part of coaching outdoors. O'Riordan and Palmer (2019) concluded in their research that 'a walk and talk outdoor coaching activity can positively influence wellbeing and vitality' (p.17).

In Shane O'Mara's book, *In Praise of Walking*, he warns that we 'overlook at our peril the gains to be made from walking, for our health, for our mood, for our clarity of mind' (2019, p.6). This is especially the case in our 'deeply unnatural environment, where we spend long periods of the day sitting with our eyes focused on screens' (p.6). We also know that walking is good for our muscles, our posture, organ protection and repair, digestion, blood flow to the brain and brain age (Carter et al., 2018). It enhances creativity, improves mood, sharpens our thinking and reduces stress. Not only that, if we look back in time, walking together to achieve a shared outcome is a genetic survival pattern for our species.

Hippocrates famously claimed that 'walking is the best medicine'. Yet in the modern world most of us spend all day sitting down. A US study showed that people spent 87% of their time in artificial built environments (Klepeis et al., 2001). Throughout history, walking has been hailed as beneficial. Aristotle is said to have taught as he walked while sharing and exploring ideas with his followers, who became known as 'peripatetic philosophers'. St Augustine, the fourth-century philosopher, is credited with the quote 'solvitur ambulando' – we solve it by walking. Ralph Waldo Emerson and Henry David Thoreau walked in the New England woods to inspire their writing. John Muir, Jonathan Swift, Immanuel Kant, Beethoven and Friedrich Nietzsche were all obsessive walkers. Nietzsche walked every day with his notebook between 11am and 1pm. He believed that all truly great thoughts are conceived by walking. Charles Dickens liked to walk the streets of London at night. Darwin walked in his garden. Jean Jacques Rousseau said: 'There is something about walking which stimulates and enlivens my thoughts. When I stay in one place, I can hardly think at all; my body has to be on the move to set my mind going' (Rousseau, 1953, p.158).

In more recent times, both Steve Jobs and Mark Zuckerberg have been known for holding meetings while walking. Barack Obama and Richard Branson walk to help with thinking and creativity. Walking changes the brainwaves waves from a beta state of wakefulness, quick thinking and multi-tasking, to a slower alpha state more akin to deep relaxation which allows for clearer thinking, problem solving and creativity. Marily Oppezzo, a Stanford University psychologist, conducted research into walking and creativity. The experiment demonstrated that creativity improved by 60% after a walk (Oppezzo & Schwartz, 2014). The changes in our brains while walking not only boost creativity but also memory. Research by Jennifer Weuve and colleagues in 2004 found that those who walked regularly had better memory and reduced cognitive decline than those that didn't.

There are economic benefits to human beings spending time in nature too. Here's a brief insight from a UK government Forest Research report. Walks taken by people in UK woodlands save £185 million a year in mental health costs. The savings come from a reduction in GP visits, prescriptions, reduced hospital and social service care, and reduced costs in lost days' work. The research also calculated that street trees cut an additional £16 million a year in anti-depressant costs (Saraev & The Forestry Commission, 2020, p.18).

Relevant Theories

We can see from all the data that we respond positively to nature. Here are two psychological theories of why this is.

Biophilia

The first theory is the Biophilia Hypothesis, which is a recurring theme throughout this book. Biophilia delves into the human relationship with nature. The concept was initially used by German psychoanalyst Erich Fromm, who described biophilia as 'the passionate love of life and of all that is alive' (1973, p.366). The idea was later expanded upon by American biologist Edward O. Wilson, who proposed that the human inclination towards nature has a genetic basis. In some cultures and individuals, there is a spiritual reverence for animals and nature. These spiritual experiences and widespread affiliation with natural metaphors (more on this in the chapter on metaphor) are rooted in the evolution of the human species, evolving in times when we had a much closer connection with the natural world than we do today. In fact, the fear that many have of spiders and snakes is thought to be an evolutionary trait from when we lived closer to nature and were more vulnerable than we are today. The same is true of a fear of thunderstorms. Those fears which initiated a fight, flight or freeze response kept us alive.

Stephen Kellert and Edward Wilson, the editors of *The Biophilia Hypothesis* book, suggest that we need a 'significant relationship with nature for our mental and physical health because we have evolved amidst a complex web of nature' (1995, p.65). We feel better and thrive in a natural environment. A meta-analysis on biophilia (taking into account 50 empirical studies) concluded that there was convincing evidence to suggest that interacting with nature resulted in positive effects on health and wellbeing (Grinde & Patil, 2009).

Attention Restoration Theory (ART) and 'soft fascination'

This second theory was developed and popularised by Stephen and Rachel Kaplan in the late 1980s and early 1990s, a time period characterised by rapid technological advancement and ever-increasing indoor entertainment.

ART proposes that through spending time in nature, our minds get a rest from the pressures of modern life and that nature has specific qualities that aid the mind's recovery process. Being in nature is not only enjoyable, but the experience brings feelings of pleasure and contentment and is restorative to our wellbeing. ART proposes that nature can also help us enhance our focus, ability to concentrate and improve our short-term memory performance (Jonides et al., 2008). Furthermore, it contends that people who spend time in nature are more intuitive, energetic and consciously attentive (Ackerman, 2020).

Kaplan (1995) talks about the experience of 'soft fascination in nature'. In urban environments, directed attention is needed while walking (e.g. avoiding traffic, looking to see where a siren noise or car horn is coming from, having our attention grabbed by advertising on billboards or shop windows), which makes the urban environment less restorative. In contrast, encounters with any aspect of the soothing natural environment – wildlife, plants, sunsets, clouds or forests – hold our attention in an undramatic fashion: soft fascination. We do not have to put any effort into attending to what we see, which has the effect of relaxing the prefrontal cortex, allowing directed-attention mechanisms a chance to replenish (Kaplan, 1995; Kaplan & Berman, 2010). This experience allows us to process internal thoughts and feelings without stimulating distraction. When we stay close to these pleasant aspects of nature, we effortlessly immerse ourselves into the experience.

Here are some thoughts to leave you with. Be it on mind, body or soul, nature leaves a lasting positive impression on every single aspect of our existence.

> Nurturing a reciprocal relationship with nature has the potential to work deeply at the intersection of many of the world's most pressing crises as well as our own personal wellness, and send us off on tangible and spiritual adventures that will last us a lifetime.
>
> (Allen, 2021, p.186)

It is not a pill or potion but consider connecting with nature as a prescription. One that works, costs nothing and has no side effects… Think of it as an opportunity to invest a bit of time in looking after yourself, your family and our planet.

Those tasked with complex organisational problems should not be cooped up in meeting rooms or on virtual calls. They should get outside in nature and walk their way to better solutions.

Activity – Wellbeing Experience

Pick a day to go for a walk somewhere green/blue. Perhaps a day when you know you'll need a break from work.

- Before you go out, take a moment to note down how you are feeling physically and mentally.
- While walking just enjoy being out. Notice what you notice both within you and around you.
- When you return, spend a few moments paying attention to how you are now physically and mentally. Perhaps note down your reflections on the same piece of paper.
- What do you notice? What have you become aware of?

Client Benefits

I took a walk in the woods and came out taller than the trees.

Henry David Thoreau (1817–1862)

I'VE SET THIS chapter out with real-life client stories of the benefits they experience from being coached outdoors. I draw out five key themes and follow this with research and explanations on what's behind their experience:

- Ease and equality from being side by side
- Supported silence offering processing time
- Clarity of thinking
- Creativity
- Perspective

 Let's dive straight in. Here is a first-hand experience a client kindly shared with me for my MSc dissertation in 2016.

This was our fifth coaching session. So far, each conversation had been focused on a business issue but this time HG wanted to talk about something personal; it was our first time outside!

HG's experience:

> I really enjoyed being coached outside; it made the whole thing more relaxing, and somehow easier to reflect and think about things. I find being outside does that. It was also easier to feel removed from the norm and focus on what we were talking about; being in an office can be distracting. Additionally, there was less concern about

being overheard. It felt more private. I found it easier to think and to talk freely and easier to focus on the task in hand. I also felt more relaxed wearing normal clothes – more natural than wearing office clothes, behaving in an office way.

The significant moment for me was sitting on the bench overlooking the water and your comment '*Just an observation, I'm hearing lots of "I"*'… I don't necessarily think it was being outdoors, or your observation, or the way I felt more relaxed, but the combination of all those things made it feel less intimidating and also made the silences for thinking feel easier. I felt it helped me to reflect on the observation and acknowledge what I was feeling. In an office, I'd have probably felt the need to fill the silence immediately with explanation/mumbling/whatever I could muster! Being outside in sunglasses helped too as I felt less exposed when I got teary; it felt less intense than it can do sitting across from one another one on one as there are other things to look at.

We can see in this example some very clear links with the wellbeing benefits in the previous chapter; for example, the experience of soft fascination and nature filling the silence. We also see new facets: the ability to make sense of things, finding reflection and thinking easier, the removal of the office 'façade' (relaxed clothes, addition of sunglasses) and the mention of changed physical positions. We unpack some of these in the rest of the chapter, starting with the change in physical positions.

Ease and Equality from Being Side by Side

As I read HG's feedback, I recognised that I had also found it easier to relax due to not having direct eye contact. King (2012, p.56) reflects how being 'alongside one another, looking in the same direction, can free us up and open up a space for a different conversation'. Liebenguth (2015, para. 12) would concur, adding: 'It is more equal, more relaxed. It allows both the coach and the client to be more comfortable with silence, which is crucial in enabling the client to reflect, to process their thoughts, to have "a-ha" moments, for ideas to flow, to feel safe to engage more deeply with themselves.' The recent research by Cook and van Nieuwerburgh (2020) into the experience of coaching while walking also cited the lack of eye contact as an experienced benefit: 'With not looking at the person you are talking to, it felt less intimidating and I felt I could talk more freely' (p.53).

Enhancing the sense of equality by physically being side by side rather than face to face has a noticeable effect on the positive experience of the client. 'Being side-by-side and having both parties facing forward, sharing a common view of the world, seems to engender a more collaborative relationship than when sat opposite each other' (Youell, 2019, p.22). The quality of the relationship between coach and client has been shown to be fundamental to successful coaching outcomes, more so than the type of theoretical intervention used (de Haan, 2008; Wildflower & Brennan, 2011).

A review of walk and talk therapy found a number of positive effects attributed to undertaking therapy while walking, including an ability to change perceptions towards relationships and feel more relaxed. As a result, clients tended to talk more freely, having greater insight, clarity and understanding. The tendency to talk more freely while walking is echoed by O'Donovan (2015), who identifies how when walking 'people tend to talk very openly and personally' (p.7). We saw this in HG's experience above and will see it again in Isaac's reflections later in the chapter.

Then there's something that many parents who have walked outdoors with their teenage children will know: 'Walking together offers a chance for conversations to evolve in ways that it couldn't, indeed wouldn't, if you simply sit together' (O'Mara, 2019, p.168).

Supported Silence Offering Processing Time

Referencing HG's mention of not needing to fill the silence, I love McGeeney's explanation of this: 'Unlike the cocktail party situation, where one can feel trapped with one other person and feel obliged to make conversation, on a walk it is socially acceptable to walk alongside someone else and not talk' (2016, p.46). I notice that for myself and my clients, this supported silence offers time for some processing, whether that's of thoughts, reflections, emotions, feelings or to assimilate what to say next. Even a few seconds of silence creates a relaxed space for the client to be with whatever is present for them at the time.

Clarity of Thinking

Next let's look at the experience that clients mention about gaining clarity while being coached on a walk outdoors. O'Mara (2019, p.147) describes his experience of clarity: 'walking allows me to zoom in on a thought, and then zoom out again, placing it in the context of other things'. Turner (2017) looked at walking as a coaching tool and found that the many benefits of walking included the natural motion of walking itself giving a connection between mind and body, enhancing thinking processes. The forward movement while walking creates a momentum, a progression experienced both physically and mentally – 'mind and body are one', which seems to help with getting 'unstuck'. As one of my clients said to me, *I often get unstuck on a dog walk*.

While all of the evidence above suggests that walking is the key to this clarity of thought, Neil Reynolds, a Mars colleague, shares: '*I unlock greater clarity of thought through the stimulating environment. I think differently.*' This suggests that the natural environment is what enhances his thinking and not necessarily the walking. Good news for those of us who like to sit outdoors for our coaching sessions!

Creativity

According to research on creativity in different conditions undertaken by Oppezzo and Schwartz in 2014 with 48 undergraduate students who were placed in a variety of settings (sitting inside; walking on a treadmill indoors;

walking outside; being pushed in a wheelchair outside), those who walked experienced increased creative ideation, with the people who walked outdoors having the highest scores. The research concluded that walking, especially in nature, opens up the free flow of creative ideas both at the time of walking and shortly afterwards. The research of Cook and van Nieuwerburgh (2020) found similar: 'Participants in this study found coaching whilst walking encouraged creativity' (p.53).

From asking my own clients, I am able to share first-hand evidence of their experience in this area and it seems that it's more than just walking that is at play here. *'Being outdoors and away from the office and home environment generates different ideas and blows the cobwebs away'* – Helen Evans, Johnson Matthey. *'As in nature, there is always a solution. I have found so many ideas generated from just stepping outside and seeing what nature offers. Mother Nature is full of ideas'* – Barry Chamberlain, Turner & Townsend. Barry's comment reminds me of Sir David Attenborough's reflections in the opening narration of *Life of Earth* (1979): 'There are four million different kinds of animals and plants in the world. That's four million solutions to the problem of staying alive.'

 I had the privilege to receive the following insights when I asked my client Isaac Fischer, Managing Director of Pukka Pies, for some reflections on what he felt the benefits of being coached outdoors were. This story reflects some of the benefits we've already covered and a few more that Isaac impactfully articulates. Isaac and I had worked together outdoors for 12 sessions at the same nature reserve.

Being coached outside was where I really started to feel the full benefit of what a coaching session could be. As soon as I step out of the car, and the fresh air hits me my mindset changes. Being outside brings with it a level of tranquility, the peace, nature, the elements – off the bat it puts me straight into a different headspace. The day-to-day front of mind issues that I am encumbered with when I am in the office, at my laptop or phone in hand somehow seem to quickly fade, as the world suddenly feels bigger, bringing with it a different, and broader, perspective.

The distractions when we are outside are positive ones. Tuning in to the sounds of the birds, squinting at the sunlight, stepping around a puddle. There is enough else going on for me not to feel the full direct intensity of the probing and challenging questions I am being asked, and getting into overthinking mode. Plus, the distractions of nature are positive wholesome ones. They don't take my head off elsewhere; if anything they ground it.

Another benefit being outside brings is the ability to walk while we talk. I feel much more natural in conversation and able to open up when we are walking side by side rather than sat opposite each other in an office. Looking out in front of me at the view, or up at the sky as we walk brings a very different dynamic from being sat opposite someone. I feel like I am still in my own headspace, and am more lucid, and probably a lot less guarded. We can discuss the most challenging topics, but walking and being outside I feel like it is just a conversation on a walk. I am a firm believer that being outdoors, and walking, makes the coaching more effective.

Finally, I feel like I have ticked multiple boxes after an outdoor coaching session. I have got some perspective back, come up with an action plan on facing into some of my most pertinent issues, I have got some fresh air, and I have got my steps in. I can come away from a good outdoor coaching session with the feeling you come away with when you have stepped out of a day at the spa or are back from a week's holiday.

As mentioned in Isaac's story, we can see again a number of benefits from coaching outdoors: the health and wellbeing benefits, relaxation, ease and equality, the experience of soft fascination, and a sense of being connected to self and the world around us. Along with an experience of perspective, the fifth coachee benefit that my clients consistently mention.

Perspective

I believe that what sits behind the perspective that clients experience when being coached outdoors is the sense of connection to the whole that I wrote about in the introduction and in the chapter on our systemic connection with nature. It's that experience of realising that we are really rather insignificant in the grand scheme of things. I conclude this from my own experience and from the following colleague and client comments: '*Coaching outdoors connects me to the bigger picture of me as a person in the universe; it helps me find perspective on issues*' – Jayne Chidgey-Clark. '*I feel small surrounded by all of this. It gives me perspective'* – SM. '*In connection with something greater than ourselves, we become more conscious of what's important to us'* – Fi Macmillan. There is definitely a biophilic strand in this but I feel there is a huge opportunity for further research here.

The perspective that clients gain outside enables them to prioritise, see the wood for the trees and focus on what really matters.

In Summary

Coaching in outdoor settings can facilitate an opening of new forms of knowing within us. Giles Hutchins and colleagues write about how working in nature helps 'integrate the coachee's different ways of knowing – intuitive, rational, emotional and somatic intelligences' (Hutchins & Storm, 2019, p.118). The benefits to the client from being coached outdoors are multi-faceted and interlinked. The main themes are that nature, movement and an enhanced coach relationship provide the foundation for a rich and valuable experience of connection, wisdom, healing, creativity, insight and spirituality.

 Activity – Client Experience

This is a lovely opportunity to ask a client for their experience of being coached outdoors. To get their perspective on what they experience.

Coach Benefits

Come forth into the light of things, let nature be your teacher.

William Wordsworth (1770–1850)

CAN BEING OUTSIDE really make that much difference to my coaching? Yes, it can. Here is clear evidence of the benefits that working outdoors brings to coaches.

While there has been no published research conducted in this area that I am aware of, the following personal experiences, from participants of our Coaching Outdoors programmes and from colleagues who have kindly shared their thoughts, provide brilliant examples of just how much of a positive effect being outdoors can have for your coaching practice.

To whet your appetite, here are three coach experiences. They capture so much in their simplicity.

> *'Working outdoors brings a joy, expansiveness and lightness of touch to my practice'* – Claire Sheldon, Coach, Supervisor.

> *'Nature held the space more than I expected. I found myself asking fewer questions, resting in the silence and following the client's intuitive experiences, allowing them to unfold organically'* – Sheryl Clowes, Coach.

> *'Coaching outside connects me to the world and helps me to be at my best; I am therefore offering my coachees the very best version of myself when I'm outdoors'* – Anon., Coach.

Key Themes

We are all humans, regardless of the label 'coach' or 'coachee', so the benefits previously discussed in the health and wellbeing chapter and the client benefits chapter will also be supporting the coach.

Other key themes that came up time and time again when I asked coaches for their experience were:

- Client connection
- Being in flow
- Congruence and authenticity
- Bravery

So, let's dive in and explore some of these benefits in greater detail.

Client Connection

Firstly, we look at the experience coaches have of being fully present and how that enhances connection with their clients. My colleague Fi Macmillan shines a light on this area with her reflection: '*I feel I am more present outdoors than when I'm inside.*' Fi cites Douglas Silsbee's definition of what being present means to her and what it offers to her clients: 'The cultivation of being characterised by the felt experiences of stillness, timelessness and connectedness' (Silsbee, 2008, p.87). Moreover, the ICF (2018) describe the 'gift of coaching presence' thus:

> With coaching presence, a coach transcends from 'doing' coaching to 'being' coaching. It allows the client to connect with a deeper self (being) from a superficial one (doing). Coaching presence also contributes to higher-order trust between the coach and the client and leads to superior and lasting outcomes.

When we read this, we can see that many of the other experiences that coaches have outside can be attributed to this sense of presence. '*I realise that I have a stronger rapport and sense of connection with those clients I have met outdoors, which builds a strong, trusting coach/client relationship*' – Sam Eddleston, Coach.

Sam goes on to say: '*I believe we get into deeper, more transformational conversations, more quickly.*' We could see this in Isaac's story in the previous chapter.

Such depth is a result of the interplay between the 'presence' of the coach and the 'presence' of nature creating an environment that enables the client to have a deeper experience, allowing them to 'know differently'. Being in nature 'seems to foster a willingness to allow an emotional or psychological shift' (Youell, 2019, p.19). This, coupled with trusting their coach, leads to a different level of disclosure compared to being indoors.

You will have noticed that rapport is also mentioned above in relation to client connection. Walking together offers a chance to deepen rapport and maintain a similar outlook. It involves coordinated movement between coach and client. We need to fall into step with one another, 'allowing us to maintain a common behavioural purpose for some period of time' (O'Mara, 2019, p.170). This synchronicity generates a feeling of connectedness, adding to the rapport between coach and client. 'Our breathing becomes synchronised… and our brains simultaneously take account of what it is that the other person is likely to do' (O'Mara, 2019, p.171). (As an aside, I have read that robots cannot achieve this, so we are free from robots taking over the coaching outdoors world for a while!) Not only are we able to take account of physically where the other person is likely to place their body while walking, we are also able to, through this deep rapport, connect with some of their internal state. In neuroscience this is explained through the action of 'mirror neurons'. 'Humans have an innate ability to sense the emotional state of those around us and to empathically mirror it at an unconscious level' (Palmer & Crawford, 2013, p.127). Lewis et al. (2000, p.63) describe the biology of this experience:

> A mammal can detect the internal state of another mammal and adjust its own physiology to match the situation – a change in turn sensed by the other, who likewise adjusts… Within the effulgence of their new brain (limbic) mammals develop a capacity we call limbic resonance – a symphony of mutual exchange and internal adaption whereby two mammals become attuned to each other's inner states.

Bearing in mind that we appear to have an easier root to our somatic awareness when we are outdoors, it is not then a surprise that coaches describe feeling closer to their client, with a deeper connection and being better able to understand them.

When walking together we have another data point and a further opportunity to communicate without actually saying anything. Walking side by side helps us to attune and get into the same rhythm as our client or, after matching their speed, to then lead the speed if we choose to. In my experience, clients often set off fast when we walk, mirroring the pace at which they have been thinking or working before arriving. Here is an illustration of exactly this experience with my client HG.

 We started walking downhill through the village to the water. I notice that HG's pace was quicker than mine. It felt directional rather than relaxed. Something that may show up in the office through speech but here, in the outdoors, it showed up physically. I was curious; I shared my observation.

'I notice you are walking quite quickly.'

'Oh yeah, I hadn't noticed, sorry. It's been a hectic day; I've been rushing from one thing to the next. It feels a bit pressurised at the moment.'

I made a choice about which avenue to take from here.

'What's been hectic-like for you?' I asked.

Damion Wonfor of Catalyst 14 shared his experience of walking with clients in one of the organisation's webinars (25 June 2019):

One of the real values that walking with people brought me was tuning into the coachee in different ways… listening more to my body as I was walking alongside them; noticing when their pace slowed down or sped up. Being curious about what that was telling me as well as the words I was hearing.

Once more, we can see that walking together and being side by side has huge benefits; in this case, the enhanced opportunity for client rapport and connection.

In Flow

'Flow' is a psychological concept described by Mihály Csíkszentmihályi in 1975. It refers to the state of peak experience of being fully immersed in something with a feeling of energised focus and enjoyment in the process of the activity. It feels effortless and 'time flies by'. We know that 'flow' leads to enhanced performance, so benefits not only the coach but also the client. Let's take a look at some coaches' experiences of this, beginning with my own.

When I coach outdoors, I find that I am more relaxed. Being relaxed seems to unlock a number of experiences for me. I am aware of and trust my intuition more. I am more curious and exploratory because I feel less pressure to get to an outcome. It's like the corporate world is far away and significantly less relevant than what really matters in life. I feel released from the perception that the client or stakeholder needs me to assist in getting to a 'solution' or 'answer'. I'm more intrigued by 'What's the enquiry? not What's the outcome' (Newell, 2015, p.3). Many other coaches I have spoken to cite being relaxed as the key to a number of benefits. *'Being away from the office always makes me feel more relaxed, more open, freer with the way that I interact with my team. It feels like such a leveller'* – Ian Stafford, Line Manager.

'I have found that being outdoors has enabled me to relax more into my coaching and bring the best of my life and coaching experience to my client. After the first ten minutes, after the environment has really had time to sink in, I find that I really get "into the flow". This enables me to be more spontaneous and creative in my coaching' – Helen Daniel, Coach

'I didn't feel under pressure to have the next question ready. I was more relaxed, just went with the flow' – A, Coach. *'The coaching conversation I had outdoors flowed more easily and the coach/coachee dynamic seemed more balanced'* – Jane Woods, Coach. Helen, Jane and the other coach above were just three of numerous coaches that mentioned 'flow'.

Feeling relaxed in nature offers the spaciousness for other things to surface or enter. We are 'open' to what we encounter; more attuned to our intuition and opportunities. In Belen's insight below, she mentions things coming naturally to her. Once again, she is not alone. Both coach and client cite 'things coming naturally' or 'feeling natural'.

> *I really enjoyed the experience of coaching someone outdoors. It felt more relaxed, less intimidating and more productive. The coachee did not need that much prompting to explore her thoughts, perceptions and ideas as they seemed to come naturally. As a coach I was able to better listen as I was able to switch off from the busy work environment and 'forget about work' for an hour. Silence and time to reflect and think felt natural. There was no urge to fill the silence.* – Belen Garcia, Coach

The sense of ease, relaxation, presence, awareness and feeling natural that coaches are aware of when coaching outdoors is part of that 'flow' experience. In turn, this creates a situation where they are at their best for their clients.

Congruence and Authenticity

Rogers (1961, p.61) believed that:

> Congruence is a way for the therapist to be true to themselves. In this state the feelings the therapist is experiencing are available to him, available to his awareness, and he is able to live these feelings, be them, and able to communicate them if appropriate.

Passmore and Marianetti state: 'Through congruence the coach facilitates psychological growth and provides the environment in which the client can flourish' (2007, p.135). It's notable that they use a nature metaphor to bring understanding! Totton believes that nature plays a role to support us in being ourselves: 'Working outdoors seems to offer a direct route to authenticity' (2014, p.14). I find that this happens more and more when I am outside. I am far more in touch with my somatic experience than when I am indoors. I find myself often saying, 'I'm noticing that I feel X'.

The experience of authenticity is not restricted to the coach. Coaches report that they *get a real version of their clients* when they are outside. That they remove the mask/façade/persona that is found in the office, and the coach can access the 'real person' more readily. We saw this in the HG vignette at the start of this chapter. Here is a further experience with HG, this time illustrating my experience of congruence and authenticity and sharing of my feelings.

 This story is taken from my unpublished MSc dissertation on 'How are we in nature and how does it shape the quality of our coaching conversations?'

Being side by side I was less conscious of how I looked – not worried about what my face was conveying, able to take more time to think and reflect, I felt I had space from the social expectations of politeness and gesture and response. I felt less responsible for the success of the conversation, I let go of control and in doing so was able to connect more fully with what was going on for me. I asked HG if she'd like to sit and enjoy the view. I was drawn to the sailboat we could see; it was gliding effortlessly across the water. We sat down together in companionable silence. Sitting on that bench with a view over the water to the boat gave me a feeling of freedom and being supported at the same time. Was it just the view and the bench supporting me that created those feelings? Or was it that we had co-created a supportive relationship in the moment? Now felt like a good moment to offer the feelings I was aware of.

The example really highlights many of the strands we have already covered coming together to create an environment where I was able to be authentic and use myself as an instrument for the benefit of the coaching session.

Bravery

Our final coach benefit theme to explore is bravery, which is closely linked to the previous theme of congruency and authenticity. I know I'm braver outside; nature supports me to say the thing that I may be thinking but which indoors I am less likely to offer due to the concern of how to land it appropriately and therefore might shy away from it or certainly sweat more about saying it. I notice when I am outside, I feel it's OK to say it.

Claire Sheldon talked about courage when I asked her about her experiences of coaching outdoors. '*What I'm increasingly aware of is feeling well supported to slow the pace right down, to be fully in the moment, and to allow not-knowing. It's easier to be courageous!*'

Here is Sam Eddleston's reflection:

> *Outdoors I feel less constrained and less conscious of any perceived hierarchy or status, which makes me more confident to challenge my client's beliefs and question their assumptions. One of my early clients held a senior position and I'm certain that indoors I would have felt rather anxious. However, for me practical outdoor clothes and walking boots are a great leveller! In stripping away our suits and office paraphernalia it feels as though we are peeling away some of the barriers, thus allowing me to be braver in what I ask.* – Sam Eddleston, Coach

Other coaches have described their bravery in taking a risk with using tools and techniques outdoors that they '*would not have gone anywhere near*' had they been inside. And the ability to say '*I'm not sure where to go next in the conversation, what would be most useful for you?*' (Anon., Coach) without the fear of being seen as incompetent.

Nature's support not only creates a safe environment for the client to 'go there' but also for the coach to be brave too.

As we have seen, with each coach benefit there is a reciprocal benefit for their client. Coaching outdoors enhances the coach's skills, in turn offering their clients a better experience and thus client outcomes. There is a vast opportunity for more research in this area. I have barely scratched the surface with what I have shared. I'm looking forward to reading and learning from the research that is sure to come.

Activity 1 – Preparation Ritual

This is a great practice to have before you meet a client outside. A short preparation ritual.

- Arrive at least 10 minutes early to the location and give yourself the opportunity to leave behind everything other than being here.
- Take three deep breaths.
- Take a 5-minute stroll, loosen up.
- Engage your senses – smell the flowers, admire the leaves, enjoy the view, touch the tree bark. Getting out of your head and into your body before they arrive.

 ## Activity 2 – Experience Reflection

When you next have a coaching session outdoors, set aside some time afterwards to reflect specifically on:

- What was your experience of being a coach outside?

Organisational Benefits

There are moments when all anxiety and stated toil are becalmed in the infinite leisure and repose of nature.

Henry David Thoreau, 1862

BEFORE JUMPING STRAIGHT into the organisational benefits, it's relevant to consider what organisations are facing and the expectations of their leaders. With this backdrop we can then consider how coaching outdoors can help. In the chapter on why coaching outdoors is growing, I wrote about the challenges business leaders are facing in today's world around demands on leadership, societal challenges, the climate crisis and global pandemics. This included how organisations increasingly need to access new ways of thinking and working to deliver different ideas and outcomes; there is a need to move fast, be agile and entrepreneurial.

In the course of my research, I spoke to a senior executive working for Mars who asked me for '*a clear compelling articulation of why we should take on the extra challenge of setting the right environment and how the extraordinary results make it a no brainer*'. We have already covered some very powerful evidence in the previous chapters on wellbeing, client and coach benefits. In this chapter we consider the specific organisational benefits of:

- Quality outputs
- Resilience
- Speed of results
- Taking others along
- Radical candour

Also as part of my research for this book, I spoke to a number of executives and key stakeholders that I have spent time working outdoors with.

You'll find their voices adding to the evidence for each of the benefits highlighted above.

When I first began offering coaching outdoors to business people in 2010, on occasion I would come up against only one concern: the commute to and from the venue. However, in the last two years, the break between the working environment (often home) and the coaching session has been seen as a positive. The coronavirus pandemic, where most people worked from home, has driven organisational trust in employees being able to make the right choices around their time and still deliver results. In fact, in recent conversations with key organisational stakeholders, they have seen the 'commute' to the outdoor sessions as a positive way of creating reflection time for their leaders. This brings us to the first of our benefits…

Quality Outputs

We've seen in the chapter on the benefits of being outdoors that our thinking slows and we become more creative outside, which in turn can support coachees to find innovative solutions to problems and have space to reflect and explore. Yvon Chouinard, founder and owner of successful outdoor clothing brand Patagonia, may not have understood the science behind the benefits of being outdoors but he inherently understood that there was value in taking his senior team to Argentina for a 'walkabout':

> In the course of roaming around those wildlands, we asked ourselves why we were in business and what kind of business we wanted Patagonia to be… We talked about the values we had in common and the shared culture that had brought everyone to Patagonia.
>
> (Chouinard, 2016, p.61)

In an era of information overload and constant demands, the ability to get some rich thinking time is a valuable resource for both the coachee or team and the organisation.

> *Getting away from a computer with an inbox and messaging service to hand made it so much easier to stay focused on the coaching. To focus on the emotional context of the challenges I was facing rather than staying at a more superficial level, which would not have been nearly as helpful. Resulting in me making true progress. So the business definitely got a greater ROI from the time spent.* – Tanja Groth, Director of Urban Resilience, SWECO

Resilience

A wealth of studies have now demonstrated that being outdoors is associated with psychological and physical wellbeing. According to Dr Matthew White of Exeter University, a brief nature fix of just 10 minutes can begin to lower our stress levels. Connecting with nature can help us feel happier and more energised, with an increased sense of meaning and purpose, as well as making tasks seem more manageable. The very thought of 'tasks seeming more manageable' is something most executives would bite your hand off for in today's world. My clients also report having a greater sense of perspective when they are outside: '*What was a big issue seems somehow diminished in the fresh air.*' And they feel more grounded. In the constant onslaught of crisis after crisis, that feeling of being grounded and retaining perspective adds to a person's resilience – worth its weight in gold for both the health of the employee and the organisation.

> *Another way of offering quality time in mental and physical wellbeing.*
> – Suzanne Coulton, COO, The INKEY List

> *Over the last two years organisations have recognised the critical importance of resilience and wellbeing in enabling individual and organisational performance and coaching outdoors brings together these key elements, providing respite/break from the usual workplace and opportunity to gain perspective and bring that back into work. I also believe that offering coaching outdoors increased loyalty through a demonstrable commitment to wellbeing and development.* – Helen Evans, Global Change Manager, Johnson Matthey

Speed of Results

In a time-poor environment, where people are looking for quick results, getting to the heart of the issue quickly and making progress is highly desirable. This happens earlier in the coaching journey when working in collaboration with nature. '*It's a short cut to the heart of the matter*' – Clare Sheldon, 2021. Now, while there is, as yet, no data-based research to validate this, a number of the coaches I have worked with have expressed their surprise at how quickly they feel their coachees have opened up about, or realised, what the 'real issue is'. They are able to have more meaningful conversations earlier in the coaching relationship than when they hold their conversations in an indoor setting.

Often in business meetings people find themselves going over old ground to reconnect people to the focus of the day because most have been too busy to do the pre-work, their cognition taken up with the latest 'burning fire' that needs putting out or the long 'to-do' list. The same is true of coaching sessions held over Zoom or in a client's office. They have just come from one meeting straight to you and are not mentally ready to connect fully with the coaching opportunity. When I meet a client outdoors, a physical and time separation from those pressures has been created by the journey to the venue. Also, as I use the same location frequently, the venue acts as an anchor back to our previous conversation, short-cutting any reconnection time. One of my clients talks about the value of being able to '*quickly reconnect with where we left off*'. Nature holds the space for the continuation of the conversation with less need for rapport building or content reminding. Once again, for the time pressured, any acceleration in connection and results is a big win.

> *Breaking the shackles of the boardroom and taking coaching conversations outdoors has far more value than I ever expected. My team have got further, faster and it has felt like an enjoyable journey rather than a meeting room slog.* – Barry Chamberlain, Director of Consulting, Turner & Townsend

Taking Others Along

Organisations highly value employees who take responsibility for driving positive change. Those people who model the way to excellence and take others with them are hugely valuable. It's one very powerful way of organically creating positive cultural change in an organisation. Such is the power and felt benefits of coaching outdoors that many line managers and leaders who experience it then cascade the experience to others in the organisation by inviting their direct reports outside for conversations too.

When I asked Nic Waller, Head of Home Furnishings for John Lewis Partnership, about the benefits of coaching outdoors she spoke about having *'walking 1-2-1s with my team, they bring dogs etc – we are both on phones – it just works – allows people to just connect in a very non-confrontational way. I can tackle some topics on a walk & talk that would be tougher face to face etc.'*

Isaac Fischer, Managing Director, Pukka Pies, shared:

> *Such was the success of being coached outdoors for the team and I, we have adopted some of the principles internally. Over the pandemic, in the windows where it was allowed, we put in place once a week walk and talk meetings for those who were home working. This was very well received.*

> *I have taken the step of doing some final-stage interviews (for senior positions) over a walk, as I feel after an hour's walk together I have a much better feeling of chemistry between me and the prospective candidate than I would spending an hour with them in my office.*

> *As a leadership team we have also committed that on a Wednesday after our team meeting we will walk in pairs on a weekly rotation, to ensure that everyone across the team is spending a level of quality time together. So far this is working well.*

Finally, under the benefit of *taking others along*, there is one more facet: the experience of nature connectedness that we covered in the 'Planet Benefits' chapter. Its relevance here is that a person who is in relational connection with nature is more likely to feel passionate about the environmental agenda and take personal responsibility for making pro-environmental choices (Mackay & Schmitt, 2019). For organisations who strive to not just talk about the environmental agenda but make active choices to change it for the better, then a leader who is passionate about this agenda, and prepared to own and role model it, is a real asset.

Radical Candour

A small caveat to this section. The description of what follows may not necessarily fall squarely into the box of 'coaching'; however, what is described is a relevant business benefit of having conversations outdoors.

In business today, as the pressure on delivering more with less and the scale and size of roles grow, it is critical that line managers are capable of having clear developmental conversations with their direct reports in a timely manner, whether that is a conversation about functional outputs or about behaviours. Both are critical in continuing to develop high-calibre employees or in quickly addressing those that are underperforming. Often these conversations are avoided because line managers shy away from something that they think is going to be difficult or challenging. Yet navigating these situations well is a defining characteristic of truly followable and inspiring leaders who build great relationships. When a manager is straightforward in saying the toughest stuff, people assume (rightly) that he or she will be brave in all kinds of essential ways: making difficult decisions, taking responsibility for them, apologising for mistakes. In other words, delivering bad news well demonstrates personal courage; it shows that you will do things that are personally uncomfortable or difficult for the good of the individual and the organisation. Kim Scott (2017) advises line managers to strive for 'Radical Candour': the ability to challenge directly and show that you care personally at the same time.

We saw in the chapter on coach benefits that being outdoors brings with it an element of bravery in the conversations we have. And you will have seen above, Nic mentions '*I can tackle some topics…*' Neil Reynolds, VP Global Digital Commerce at Mars Wrigley gave a great perspective on the impact for line managers and leaders of taking their coaching conversations outdoors: '*It unlocks the power in all of us as coaches. Coaching outdoors "feels" more conversational and natural despite what may be a tough topic. It increases the confidence of all associates to face into those topics often avoided in the office.*'

In Summary

We can see that coaching outdoors is an incredibly powerful way of helping leaders and executives manage some of the pressure of the working world today. It offers so many benefits in one place: health and wellbeing benefits, both physical and mental; possible environmental benefits; the benefits that the coachee experiences and those that are there to be capitalised on from an organisational perspective. So, the return on investment (ROI) both of money and time stack up well. Coaching outdoors offers a new way of working for faster, multi-faceted results. Where appropriate, it would almost be difficult to argue for having coaching sessions in the office ever again.

Section III

Get Started Coaching Outdoors

Psychological Safety

THE TERM PSYCHOLOGICAL safety was originally coined by Schein and Bennis (1965). It refers to being able to be yourself, take risks and be vulnerable without any negative consequences. It's about feeling safe.

So, what does that mean for coaches, and in this context, coaches that work outdoors? In this section I look at when not to go outdoors, how our past experiences can influence our time outside, choosing the optimum location and working with groups.

When Not to Go Outdoors

You may hear the following words of caution, as I did in 2014 when I was discussing my action research dissertation on coaching outdoors with some of my professors and cohort:

'It's not always safe.'

'Have you considered the ethics of being outdoors?'

'Are you sure all your clients are comfortable outside?'

'People may not feel safe.'

When I asked my peers if they'd coached outdoors, most said no. However, there is value in examining their words of caution because sometimes it is inappropriate to be outside, as this case study highlights.

> I was with some Ashridge peers involved in a group coaching exercise. The sun was shining and we were next to a beautiful outdoor space. My suggestion of going outside was met with a definite *'No'*

from one of the group so we held our session indoors. I found it hard to understand why anyone would not want to go outside on such a gorgeous day. Aware of my research, I realised I might have a blind-spot so I said nothing more but resolved to expand my perspective after the session. When we finished, I enquired of the participant: '*What was it about going outdoors that meant you wanted to stay in?*' She replied: '*I wanted a safe container for the conversation, somewhere for us to be held.*' She went on to explain that being in a room felt more secure for her than being outdoors. That the conversation would be contained. Others in the group contributed that a room provided intimacy and boundaries. I was curious to know if it was important all the time for her to be indoors. '*Do you like all your coaching sessions to be inside? Or are you happy to be outside on occasion?*' '*Outside is lovely sometimes; it just depends on how I am feeling and on the topic.*'

My learning from this was to, if appropriate, offer an outdoor coaching session; however, accept a '*no*' from the client and be aware of the balance of 'power' (Bergen et al., 2006) in the coaching relationship that generally lies with the coach!

Listening to Intuition

I'd like to share another case study with you, this time with a corporate team where my 'felt sense' (Gendlin, 1982) was a guide in my bid for psychological safety.

A month, and a number of sessions outdoors after the Ashridge vignette above, I was working with a leadership team at a venue that I had specifically chosen for its outside space. Our focus for the event was the team's leadership identity and we were exploring the experiences in life that have shaped who we are today. This was a senior leadership team I'd worked with previously outdoors and we'd agreed that a venue which was relaxed and informal would create the right environment for some personal reflection and exploration. While I was setting up for the day, I kept checking the outside space. There was something not quite right about it: too open, too noisy (road traffic), not private enough. I felt uncomfortable about using it with the group as I couldn't relax while I was out there.

I felt unsafe and exposed; I couldn't conceive how this space would provide the safe, and relaxed environment I hoped for. Each time I came back inside I felt a sense of relief. The room felt cosy, contained and safe. I decided to listen to my intuition and held the session inside. We used the outdoors space for breaks and lunch.

I don't know how the day would have evolved if we'd been outdoors, but I do know that on that day, at that venue, I was a better coach indoors than I would have been, feeling exposed, outside! Our somatic awareness is invaluable in coaching. I don't always hear mine, but it seems to shout louder to me when I work with nature and it provides me with a great source of insight. We take a look at this in greater detail later.

Chemistry Sessions

There is one other time when, as a rule, I don't go outdoors, and that's for chemistry sessions. These confidential conversations between coach and potential client are designed for each party to get to know each other a little bit, build rapport and explore if you are a good match for each other. The client wants to establish the following: *'Do I feel safe with this coach, un-judged, listened to and can I be open with them? Does this coach seem credible and can they help me?'* The coach wants to know if they can be of service for the client or if someone else might serve them better. The chemistry session also helps clarify and set the expectations for outcomes, ways of working and processes.

There are so many unknowns at this stage in the relationship that an indoor venue or a virtual connection provides a safer and less committing container for this first meeting. One of the fundamental elements of the chemistry session is the ability to establish rapport between coach and coachee. Not only does being inside together or in a virtual meeting allow more eye contact; it also provides more visual information on which to base our decision. The side-by-side nature of being together outdoors (which of course does have many benefits) does not allow for this foundation to be established. And that's just eye contact; the chemistry session also provides the opportunity for an enquiry about the possibility of working outdoors. Create the chance to discuss this option with the client and understand how they feel about it before finding yourself outdoors with someone in summer who has a hay fever allergy!

Being inside/virtual for a chemistry session also ensures there is one less unknown for the client in the initial meeting. You are on more even ground (pardon the pun) if you are both in an environment you are familiar with.

Finally, when we are outdoors, we are in a three-way relationship with nature. It would be like bringing a friend along to a first date! Not an ideal situation for finding out if the two of you get on.

Our Past Experiences

Life is full of past experiences and things that have meaning for us. When we step outside the risk of encountering 'triggers' is far higher than in a 'cleaner' indoor setting. We cannot cover all our bases and mitigate for everything that may be a triggering event and in fact there is often richness to be found that adds value to the coaching conversation if you do encounter one. Here are a couple of simple trigger examples: '*Kingfishers are very special for me. It is a good omen if I see one*' – coaching client, 2020. I was unaware of the king-fisher importance to my client until she volunteered that she'd seen one on a self-coaching walk. I didn't enquire into the story that lay behind it, but I did make a mental note in case we saw one (unlikely) when we were together. Another client believes that her deceased father is by her side when she sees a robin. Once I knew this, I was able to contract with her on how she would like us to manage the situation in the highly likely event we'd come across one when out on our walks. While my examples have both been of animals, they could just as easily have been flowers or smells.

Landscapes too have an evocative power. Ronen Berger, nature therapist, describes his surprise at discovering that his clients had different attitudes and relationships with a variety of landscapes: 'I learned that I cannot predict what reaction, memory, or image a person will bring up in any given land-scape' (Berger, 2007, p.42). Nick Totton highlights the same learning in his book *Wild Therapy*: 'it became clear that people are influenced by different [location] characteristics, including not only their feelings and sensations but also the memories they evoke, their way of thinking, and the metaphors they encounter' (Totton, 2011, p.160).

As an outdoor coach I am curious about what relationship my clients have with nature and where that has come from. For example, has it been a sooth-ing partner medicating some kind of human relational gap? Has it been a place of excitement and adventure for someone's 'free child' (Berne, 1964)?

Or has it been a place of danger and loss? With this type of enquiry, we can also begin to build a picture of where nature sits in someone's psychic structure, i.e. where it sits as part of their protective defence system. For example:

> I thought back to where I felt most comfortable during difficult periods in my own life… Outdoors among trees and in parks. Nature became what I thought of as a 'universal parent' in the way it guided, carried and nurtured me with its presence… Walking in nature gave me clarity, and the space to listen to myself. It didn't judge or distract, and it connected me with my environment and my feelings.
>
> (Hoban, 2019, p.1)

You can begin to see how our clients' past experiences of being outdoors can affect how they feel and behave in nature and that in our coaching role it is important for us to pay attention to this. Then there's your experience of being in nature. In Section IV we consider what is your history of being outdoors and with various different types of landscape? And how much of that do you bring with you into your coaching work outdoors?

Location

I look at location more closely later in this chapter. Here we consider location with specific reference to psychological safety.

> The physical locations in which we meet our clients can greatly affect our chances of engaging in a person-to-person encounter. Physical spaces tend to 'set the scene' quite literally, with their symbols of power, hierarchy, detachment or, conversely of closeness, informality, openness.
>
> (King, 2012, p.56)

Here's Berger (2007, p.42) bringing to life for us what King says above: 'working in a shaded forest will create a different atmosphere than working in a hot desert, and working on a windy morning on the beach will foster different progress than working on the same beach under the moonlight'.

What might be overwhelming for one client may be just what another needs both in terms of the 'feeling' the environment creates and the metaphors available. Just imagine the enquiry potential for someone who is wanting to get unstuck and become future focused, to have expansive space that invites movement and a view that encourages thoughts on journeying. Yet the same space could be overwhelming for a client who is already feeling fragile, they may require an enclosed space to feel held more tightly. A walled garden, for example, provides a safe environment free of surprises and with a good line of sight to the one entrance/exit and the opportunity to sit on a bench with your back to a solid brick wall.

Berger (2007, p.41) describes location choice both in terms of what it offers to the client and in what it may trigger: 'The impact of the choice of space on the process made me understand... how considered choice of setting is a crucial part of the planning work.' This links to the previous experiences dynamic. For example:

> I walk through forests and woods in trepidation as it's often here that I fear that I will lose my way. I also find when looking upwards close to the huge trunks of conifer trees that my stomach quivers. I've almost not got the 'bottle' for forests.
>
> (Author unknown)

One final area for consideration with regard to location choice: perhaps your coachee has a fear of cows/sheep/dogs, etc. It's useful to enquire about this at the contracting stage because once you know this you can choose locations where they will feel safe; however, if you don't know and you come across animals your client is afraid of, they will feel unsafe and have their capacity for a good coaching conversation reduced significantly! However, we cannot hope to manage every eventuality and it would not be natural if we did. Instead, I invite you to become aware of how your choice of setting can influence much of what takes place in the process, to recognise that location choice has many more layers than perhaps we first consider; it can provide rich opportunities, but can also be a Pandora's Box! It goes way beyond ensuring there is suitable parking and toilets!

Other Considerations

As we saw in the benefits chapters, for some clients one of the main elements of psychological safety that nature offers is the ability to be beside their coach and not to have the discomfort of constant eye contact or even the need to make any eye contact, and so they feel less 'exposed'. Then there is the safety that comes from not having any pressure to say anything at all – the feeling that silence is acceptable. '*I use this venue now for conversations. I find it freer, less intense, no need to make conversation, the landscape fills the gaps, I feel more comfortable*' – coaching client, 2021.

And a psychological safety consideration on a delicate subject… During one of the Nature as Co-Facilitator programmes I run, a male coach raised the consideration: '*I'm not sure how comfortable I am/my coachee is if we're an hour away from anywhere and they're a woman.*' It's not something I'd considered before and I have not had personal experience of this. As a group we discussed it and came to the conclusion that the concern could be mitigated through the contracting process and, if needed, careful selection of location and completion together of the risk assessment form that can be found in the appendices.

Thoughts to Leave You With

Some of the situations above we can plan for; others we cannot. Please don't be put off by the numerous variables. Just as you will have strategies for managing unexpected emotions within an indoor coaching setting, you will, with planning, equip yourself with strategies to manage the turn of events in an outdoor coaching session.

And remember: 'It would seem that many people coming for outdoor therapy experience the natural world as a less pressurized relational space essentially comprised of undemanding others' (Marshall, 2016).

It's lovely to get out here and get away from the office, to look at the view and get perspective. I feel stronger and more alive just by being outside.
H. Greenwood, coaching client

 Activity – Plan for a Client Session

1. What new considerations or questions might you now have for each of your coaching clients?
2. What strategies will you employ to manage the unexpected?
3. With a client in mind, consider a location that you think might support them well. Visit that location and tune in to the following:
    • How do you feel here?
    • What does it offer you?
    • What might it offer your client?
    • In what ways could you work in partnership with the landscape?

Contracting

Opportunity arises for the prepared mind.

Louis Pasteur, 1854

THREE-SIDED, FOUR-SIDED, PSYCHOLOGICAL, hidden – so many contracts. Let's start with a quick recap of the basics before we look at the specifics for coaching outdoors.

A contract – the rules of engagement/agreements that are made between:

- Coach and client
- Or coach, line manager and client (three-sided)
- Or coach, line manager, HR/the business and client (four-sided)

The aim of a contract is to agree on a number of factors that coaches and their clients will align on. Eric Berne (1910–70), the founder of Transactional Analysis, elegantly described a contract as 'an explicit bilateral commitment to a well-defined course of action'. Berne talked about three areas of contracting:

1. Administrative – timings, fees, venue, logistics etc.
2. Professional – purpose and proposed outcomes.
3. Psychological – clarifying expectations, thoughts and assumptions. Not always tangible and constantly evolving.

The contract for a coaching engagement cannot be assumed; it must be dealt with explicitly before the coaching relationship begins. Having a contract that fits the purpose (provides the right container for the conversation without getting in the way) is a crucial piece of work. It is also ethical to revisit contracts to ensure they evolve along with the coaching work.

Spending the time to set a robust contract creates an ideal opportunity to engage the sponsor fully with setting the coaching goals, designing the evaluation criteria and exploring their role in supporting the coachee to succeed. This last element frequently takes line managers or stakeholders aback when I ask it; they are often unsure as to how they are going to support the coachee in making progress. I have found it is a good provocation! Finally, when coaching outdoors, you could also include into your contracting a measure for the impact that the coachee felt being outside in nature had for them. It provides great evidence for the incremental benefits of coaching outdoors!

What's Different About a Contract for Coaching Outdoors?

Well, all the same contracting principles apply as with a normal coaching engagement. However, what must also be included is an element in the administrative/logistics section around being outdoors. It begins with an initial conversation with the client agreeing that they would like to work outdoors. (A little consideration here: is your client happy to work outdoors or have you persuaded them into it? It's tempting when we know the huge benefits for us to drive the agenda too far and for them to feel that they have to say yes when actually they would rather say no. Remember, the coaching is to serve them, not your agenda.)

In this initial contracting conversation, I assure the client that the walk is secondary to the conversation – an easy stroll on paths. We agree roughly what distance they are comfortable with. I have found that, in general, 4–7km is good – client, terrain and weather dependent. I also highlight that there are options to extend the walk or shorten it, have a sit down along the way and there is always the option not to walk if they change their mind when they arrive. Each of these choices gives the client more control over the environment they are being coached in and is an important element of ensuring they feel psychologically safe. Finally, I ask the client if there is any health condition that it would be useful for me to be aware of, such as an allergy to bee stings, hay fever, diabetes or musculoskeletal concerns. We agree how these will be managed and that it is the client's responsibility to flag any concern in this area at any time. In the appendices there is a sample risk assessment form from my colleague Sam Eddleston. It is a super tool to make sure you've covered all the bases.

A couple of days before each coaching session, as part of the 'sessional contract' (Sills, 2006), I share a brief weather update. I also mention if I am taking gloves, a hat, a waterproof, sun cream, water bottle, etc. depending on what the weather is predicted to do. I do this to support the coaching conversation, not to play mum. I know the locations well and how they feel in various weather conditions; my intention is for clients to be able to focus on the coaching and not be concerned about being too hot or having wet socks! So, you can see that the dynamic nature of the sessional contract increases when coaching outdoors. I have also learnt not to assume that just because a client has worked outdoors with me before, that they will want to every time; they may have different needs on different days.

Here's the **checklist** I use to make sure I cover everything:

- ✓ Location and route choice communicated.
- ✓ Weather forecast shared.
- ✓ Sharing clothing or kit choices.
- ✓ Risk assessment completed.
- ✓ Car parking and toilet facilities informed.
- ✓ Quick nod to general health – anything I need to know?

The Best-Laid Plans...

With almost every client I have worked with outdoors, we have had at least one session indoors. Each time the reason has been different: weather, Covid-19, client choice, injury, emotions; the list is long and varied. We have ended up in a variety of places: a country pub garden, in the same pub by a blazing fire, the quiet lounge of a 5* hotel and over Zoom. It is the coach's responsibility to be prepared for this and to have a suggested back-up that can be agreed at short notice. In the initial contracting, clients should be aware that this is an option as it is a contributing factor towards their psychological safety.

Confidentiality

Whether in a meeting room, a local park, a country pub or a hotel, we must pay attention to confidentiality. There will be the standard element of confidentiality that is in your normal contract and the consideration for what you agree is shared back with the organisation.

When coaching outdoors, we also need to consider that the conversation may be overheard by people you walk past or perhaps the people who are having morning coffee in the country pub or café you are using as an alternative venue due to the heavy rain outside. As with all contracting, the key is to have a conversation about it and agree what your client is comfortable with, recontracting in the moment if necessary.

In summary, there are some special additions to the normal coaching contract; the key is to be aware of them, discuss them and agree how they will be mutually managed.

 Activity – Agreeing a Contract

So by now I'm sure you're inspired to give coaching outdoors a go.

- Which of your current clients do you think coaching outdoors would be a good option for?
- What questions will you ask them to explore if they'd like to take the next session outdoors?
- What plans will you put in place?
- What recontracting will you do?

Location, Location, Location

There is pleasure in the pathless woods. There is rapture on the lonely shore. There is society where none intrudes, by the deep sea and music in its roar. I love not man the less but nature more.

Byron, 1824

NATURE ENCOMPASSES ELEMENTS and phenomena of the Earth's land, water and biodiversity – from a pot plant, small stream or park to expansive, pristine wilderness with its dynamic of weather and geology. So, from office grounds to Ben Nevis – where is the most appropriate space for coaching outdoors? Well, it depends…

Where are you and your client going to be most physically comfortable? What location is going to serve as the best container to meet the need of the client and their current issue? Where is going to provide a psychologically safe space?

Physical Comfort

A coaching session's focus should be on the conversation and not on the challenge of walking. If your or your client's capacity is taken up with physical exertion, way-finding or managing a fear of sheep, cows, birds or heights, then you are not offering a supportive environment or psychological safety.

It is important that you know your comfort zone and boundaries and those of your client so that you work within them (unless it complements the client's development to work at the edge of their boundary and you've contracted to do so). For many people their comfort zone will be a low-level walk on a firm path; for a handful of others it might be mountainous terrain.

Due to my participation in the Clipper Round the World Yacht Race, I'm often asked about running coaching sessions on boats for individuals and teams. I can honestly say that unless you are both (or all, if it's team development) very accomplished sailors or you are spending a few consecutive days on a development journey and are able to get comfortable at sea, then the environment is not going to support the work. Much of my attention during my first few weeks at sea was taken up with *'I hope I'm not seasick'*, *'what does this rope do?'*, *'what were we told about winches?'*, *'I don't want to lose my finger in this one'*, *'make sure I don't get hit by the boom'*, *'what if I do something wrong?'*, *'where's the best place to stand/sit?'*, *'how do I go to the toilet and how does it flush?'*. My capacity was consumed with staying safe and managing my insecurities at sea. I had nothing left for reflection, awareness and exploration of my patterns, behaviours, thoughts, feelings and assumptions. Six months later after being at sea 24/7, it was a different story; sailing was sub-conscious and I would have been in a great place to have been coached at sea, not least because I felt alive and free on the ocean.

While a racing yacht is an extreme example, it helps to paint a picture of how important it is to stay within your and your client's comfort zone, allowing your full attention, at every level, to be focused on the coaching session.

The Right Container

The qualities of the natural setting you choose can determine the impact of the session for a client. For example, a small shady woodland area enclosed by trees can feel private, intimate and containing – especially good for emotional fragility. Open downs with their vast expanse of sweeping space, few trees and long views can feel much more exposing and uncontained – perhaps overwhelming for a client who is feeling particularly vulnerable. However, if a client is wanting to shift perspective and unstick something then a space that invites freedom and movement can be supportive. A horizon is great for conversations about the future. Water is great for reflection. Being close to a river, stream or pond is also great to support accessing emotions. When we connect emotionally our eye gaze is drawn down; looking at moving water can begin this accessing process.

Nature offers so much in the way of supporting us. As coaches we have an opportunity to become attuned to this and to match the client's needs with the best environment, thus allowing nature to make a positive contribution to the dynamic created for the client.

Green Space/Blue Space

'Green space' and 'blue space' have popped up as terms for trees and grass, and water. I'm often asked if one is better for coaching than the other; well (you'll not be surprised!), it depends... Both are highly restorative natural environments (Barton & Pretty, 2010; Gladwell et al., 2013). As far back as the 18th century, medics were prescribing convalescence by the sea, but it's only been in the last decade that evidence for a 'blue health' effect has emerged, with studies showing that people who live close to the coast tend to have better health and higher life satisfaction than those who reside inland (World Health Organization, 2021). Data suggests that people in the UK tend to be happiest when they are by the coast, and research has directly pitted green spaces (like the countryside) against rivers, lakes and the ocean. Blue spaces repeatedly come out on top (World Health Organization, 2021). However, being by the sea is not logistically possible for most coaching sessions. So, while we may not be achieving the greatest possible benefit by walking through a London park while we have our coaching conversation, we are definitely creating a better opportunity for health and wellbeing than sitting in an office.

White et al. (2013) and Albert et al. (2014) have shown that the greener the urban space, the lower the mental distress and the higher the wellbeing experience. Extrapolated, this would suggest that the further along the continuum we move from urban to wild, the more we benefit.

If you have access to both then you could ask your client for their preference or, as discussed in the section above, choose the environment that you feel serves the issue best. The holy grail would be to have green and blue in one location with a variety of route options.

What Makes a Good Location?

It depends. There are some fundamentals listed below but let's begin by considering our personal histories. What is your experience of each type of location; what does it evoke for you? There is an opportunity in location choice to choose a setting that you can really connect with, 'as in many

ways the therapist's relationship with the place is as significant as the client's'
(Marshall, 2016). Allowing the landscape to 'hold' the client and to 'hold'
you offers a sense of freedom to you both. '*I observed that different outside
space can have a different impact on me; when I was coaching by the water, I felt
significantly calmer and more in the moment than I did when I coached in the
park*' – Amand Nelson, Coach. What do the outdoor locations you coach
in offer you? Here's an excerpt from my dissertation that highlights how I
experience one of the locations I work with:

> In this tiny village, surrounded by water, fields and trees, I felt safe
> and protected from the pressures of life, held by this place of sanc-
> tuary. I was present and focused, in the 'moment'. And interestingly
> here are my client's reflections from the same location; 'I feel so
> lucky to be in such a beautiful place. I ought to get out here more
> often just to "be"'.
>
> (Roberts, 2016, p.33)

If you use a location regularly with a variety of clients you begin to notice
patterns that can be a rich source of insight; the bench that people are drawn
to, the tree they comment on, the moments when the conversation takes
a turn from head to heart, or their walking relaxes. A regular location also
enables you to consider how different clients respond to the variety of stimuli that nature offers. I am a big fan of knowing your location and what it
can offer both the client and yourself. For example, on my usual coaching
route at Rutland Water, we turn along a quiet country road bordered by

fields on our way back to the car. This is my 'Columbo Moment'; I signal that we are almost back and ask my clients *'is there anything else you wanted to talk about today?'* On many occasions, this has added real value to the session as it has brought up the 'thing' they've been hanging on to! With my knowledge of the route, I time that question to give us enough of an opportunity to explore something additional if we need to.

And the fundamentals – there are some very simple logistical basics that the venue you choose for coaching outdoors must have:

- Access to a toilet nearby
- Parking or public transport
- Shelter if the weather turns
- A reasonable amount of peace and quiet

And then there is the icing on the cake:

- A mix of woodland, water, open space and good views
- Seats along the way
- The ability to lengthen and shorten the walk
- The chance to pick a different route to stay out of the wind/sun
- Having a variety of walks in the same location
- Wildlife and interesting features that you can draw on
- Awe inspiring

I realised having gone back to a location that I love to walk in that it would not work with clients. When I went with my coaching hat on, I noticed the paths were not wide enough and it was full of loud pre-schoolers. – Getting Started Coaching Outdoors programme participant, 2022

There is a handy checklist at the end of this chapter which includes these elements. It will help you with your location choice.

What About the Travel Time?

Within reason, of about an hour's travel to the location, clients have told me they appreciate the travel time to the session. It offers them a buffer from day-to-day pressures. They use the journey there to let go of the office pressures and to gather their thoughts for the session ahead, while the journey back, or ideally home, allows for settling and reflection before other demands are placed upon them. Kolb's (1984) learning cycle suggests that interventions need to build in sufficient space for reflection. You don't get this protected time when coaching in an office environment. Clients are often rushing from meeting to meeting, arriving at best distracted, at worst distraught and late. Then they leave their coaching session straight into the next meeting with no time for digestion.

> *The danger is it becomes just another hour block in an already full schedule. I roll off a call about a particular business issue, straight into a coaching session, and then straight back into business issues. There is a level of overhang from events preceding it, and distraction is prompted by the events proceeding it. I carry the intensity of work mode into the coaching session, and no sooner have I settled my mindset than I am ramping back up again.* – Client, IF

> *I appreciate the protected time that meeting here offers me. It's so peaceful having some thinking time in the car and space away from the laptop and meetings. I've hardly had any of that since Covid. I also really appreciate going home to the kids straight from here. I'm more relaxed when I arrive and ready to be with them instead of my head being filled with work stuff.* – Client, HE

> *The drive here and back is a lovely period of time just for me, protected from all the pressures of the office. I spent my drive here looking forward to this and thinking about what I really wanted to get from our time. The drive back will give me an opportunity to reflect and have some space for me, rather than go straight into the next meeting.* – Client, JS

Unknown Venues

What if your coachee suggests you meet at a venue you don't know? Or the place that is most convenient for both of you is one you have not been to? Well, it's a personal choice. This has occurred for me on a few occasions and sometimes it has worked out well and other times not so well. On one occasion I met a client at Clumber Park in Nottinghamshire, a beautiful location which I would use again: plenty of parking, lots of space, water and trees, wide open paths and a variety of routes. It was ideal. However, I was not as fully focused on the client as I could have been due to not knowing the venue (perhaps that says something about a need for control!). Part of my attention was taken with making sure we didn't get lost or end our session miles away from where we had started; there were also route decisions to make along the way. No one would necessarily hold me responsible for any of these decisions but I felt, as the coach, that I had a duty of care for my client. With hindsight, I could have approached this differently – as an opportunity for contracting around how we would manage these questions.

On another occasion, I found myself in a park in the middle of Sheffield and while it provided some beautiful features – stepping stones, secluded paths, grand trees, a pond with ducks and some well-placed benches – it was in the middle of town and was not a very large area so I felt I was walking in circles and avoiding people and traffic. I found myself getting frustrated and therefore was not at my best as a coach.

Other coaches I've worked with experience unknown venues differently. They say it 'levels the playing field', taking away the 'power' (Bergen et al., 2006) that comes from knowing the venue and that this has had a positive impact on the coaching session.

It's all about knowing what supports you to give your best to each client.

Portfolio of Locations

Just as coaches excel in flexing to meet the needs of clients, you can see that by having a variety of walks to draw on you can meet both your and the client's location needs (physical capability and preference, geography, weather, psychological safety, etc.), giving you the best chance of a valuable session.

Have fun beginning your walk portfolio and don't forget to take a map if it's a location you don't know very well. I love UK Ordnance Survey maps and they now come digitally as well as the old-fashioned paper copy (although I prefer paper!).

Woodlands, riverside walks, meadows, nature reserves, national parks, canal walks and city parks. The world's your oyster; have fun exploring what works for you.

Does it Feel Right?

And just like buying a house, there is also the 'hard-to-put-your-finger-on' sense of how it feels. Does it feel right? I was exploring a walk one day as a possible route to use with a client and instead of feeling awed by nature and gently relaxed, I felt uncomfortable, unsafe and a bit 'spooked'. Now I'm not really one for 'other worldly' things but there was definitely something about the location that felt odd so I know it is not a supportive environment for my work and I won't use it. Trust your intuition as well as your checklist of criteria.

 Activity – Explore a Location

So, let's go for a walk.

Pick a location you'd like to use for a coaching session and go for a walk.

- What did you notice?
- How did you feel in that location?
- What does it offer you?
- What might it offer a client?
- Is it one for your portfolio of locations?

Location Checklist

Car parking/public transport links ☐

Toilets ☐

Alternative venue nearby if the weather is bad ☐

Route options ☐

Appropriate route length ☐

Know how long the walk takes ☐

Benches/sit spots ☐

Good-quality paths (to save muddy feet or twisted ankles) ☐

Paths wide enough to walk side by side ☐

Woodland ☐

Good views ☐

Wildlife ☐

Water ☐

Know where to find shelter if it rains ☐

Quiet enough ☐

Does it feel good? ☐

© J. L. Roberts

Weather

A change in the weather is sufficient to recreate the world and ourselves.

Marcel Proust (1871–1922)

IN THIS CHAPTER we look at important considerations around weather. If you are living in the UK, you will have noticed that our changeable weather dominates a large part of polite daily conversation and that's mainly from people who work indoors. Imagine the considerations for those working outdoors! Weather can have a huge impact on how we feel and everyone responds differently to the elements – from people finding storms frightening to others who find them elemental and energising. Here we explore finding your boundaries in weather, contracting with client around theirs and being prepared. The key is for the weather not to distract or to get in the way of the coaching experience for either coach or client.

Comfort Zones

Weather is rarely as bad as it looks: *'bad weather always looks worse through a window'* (Tom Lehrer). However, the critical considerations are: how comfortable am I in this weather? Is my coachee comfortable? And, do I have a back-up location? People may say *'there's no such thing as bad weather, just the wrong clothing'* and Billy Connolly would add that we should *'get a sexy wee raincoat and live a little'*. However, that's no good for coaching if, being physically uncomfortable as a result of the weather (or anything else for that matter), you are unable to give your full attention to the client and the coaching work.

Making sure you are in your comfort zone and will not be distracted by the weather is a key consideration to having a successful coaching session. Everyone is different: one person may be very happy in the rain but unhappy in the wind; someone else may love the heat, while yet another may feel faint in hot sunshine. Our role as coaches is to be in service of our clients. If you are distracted by trying to stay dry or warm, your client is being denied some of your attention. Any capacity taken up with personal concern for comfort is getting in the way of what you have available to support your coachee.

To ensure this does not happen: firstly, know your comfort level, not tolerance, that's different (we can tolerate far more than we are comfortable with). Then, check with your client what they are happy with. Beware the 'power' (Clarkson, 2000; Wampold, 2001; Kilburg, 2004; O'Broin & Palmer, 2006) that you have as a coach to lead people. Tread lightly when contracting around weather and what others are comfortable with and trust your intuition; it's usually right.

 What follows is a vignette from a client I worked with called Richard. It is a good example of knowing comfort levels and making choices based on them. We were due to meet at Curbar Edge in the Peak District:

It was November but not too cold. I'd checked the weather and knew it was going to be pretty wet and windy. It had been raining for the previous few days and I was beginning to have my doubts about the location. I emailed Richard to share my concern and he said he was still happy to go out; as he'd suggested the location, I didn't feel I was leading him in any way. On our previous coaching session, we'd had a conversation about being outdoors triggered by the jacket he was wearing; it was a technical mountaineering waterproof (Rab brand) and I'd commented on it. He said he loved walking and often spent whole weekends outside between long walks with his family and endurance bike rides.

As I drove to Curbar Edge the rain began, a constant drizzle on a grey day. I arrived at the car park and wondered if we should find a cosy quiet place for our conversation. Curbar Gap runs along a crag top and is very exposed with nowhere to shelter. I was weighing up my comfort level with the weather and considering how it would impact the conversation. I eyed up my waterproofs on the back seat and wondered whether or not to don my waterproof trousers as well as jacket. Before I could decide, Richard arrived. OK, I thought, before I get 'all togged up' (and inadvertently pressure him into walking because I look like I'm ready), I'm going to check that he still wants to walk '*in this*'. Before I got to his car, he'd opened the door and was smiling and pulling on his jacket.

'Are you sure you want to go for a walk in this?' I asked.

'Definitely, I've been looking forward to it,' came his response.

I pointed out, *'I'm not sure the rain is going to stop and I suspect it's going to be pretty muddy and slippy underfoot, are you OK with that?'*

'Ah, yeah, it'll be fine; I've got good walking stuff and we'll soon dry out. I've been looking forward to this walk; I really need to get outside and clear my head.'

I walked back to my car to get my waterproofs and hat. Unhelpfully I found I'd forgotten my hat and had to make do with my daughter's; she's 5 and her hat has two pompoms on the top! Joking aside, it was a big lesson for me. I hate having wind in my ears and I found myself having to work hard throughout the walk not to get distracted by the fact that the hat did not cover my ears. I am pretty comfortable in most weather conditions so it was a revelation to me how distracting it was to be uncomfortable.

Our walk was slippy, grey, windy and wet the whole way. Richard was well within his comfort zone and relished the elemental nature of the walk for clearing his head. For most it would have been fairly miserable, and an indoor venue would have been a more resourceful choice.

That day with Richard was a real insight for me into how important it is to be properly equipped if you do choose to go out in inclement weather. For you, the story may have caused you to consider your or your clients' 'comfort zone'.

Windy Weather

The main considerations in wind are safety from falling branches and being able to hear properly. Not hearing your client and constantly asking them to repeat themselves, or them not hearing your reflections and questions, does not make for a relaxed session; instead it creates a battle! So, if it's windy, it's not 'don't go out'; it's 'pick your location and route carefully'. Often it is possible to find shelter from the wind in woods, or to walk in the lea of the land or trees, allowing your session outdoors to go ahead.

Here's an extract from my coaching diary on a windy day:

It's Tuesday, it's windy, wet and grey. I have a client booked for an outdoor coaching session tomorrow, this weather is not ideal! I check the weather for the following day; Sunshine – yes. Dry – yes. Windy!!!!! OK so we can still go out I just need to give some thought to our route. Somewhere sheltered would be ideal.

I pick a route which has quite a lot of woodland paths, is low lying and I can choose our direction of travel so that the wind is at our backs in the more exposed sections. I email the client to give them a quick weather update, check they are still happy with the plan and mention that I'll have a hat on. On the day I pop out for a short walk in the morning – Just how windy is it? Will it be too distracting? It seems ok.

I'm really clear that while I'm not put off by less than perfect weather, I want my client and myself to be able to focus on our conversation and not to be focused on battling the wind. During the session I did notice the wind for the first 5 minutes but it soon disappeared partly due to us warming up, partly to our quick descent down the hill at the start of the route and partly because the coaching conversation became the focus as we moved out of the wind.

Warm and Sunny

Glorious sunny days bring a relaxed holiday feel. It's key to ensure everyone has water available. Either take some along for your coachee or drop them a message asking them to bring a bottle for the walk. Shade will be an all-important consideration on your route choice. Then there's sun cream and hats; while not wanting to be parental (Berne, 1964), I do feel that given we often know the route and length of time outside, it is considerate to mention sun cream and hats to clients.

My supervisor (with whom I have a well-established relationship) is particularly good at contracting around weather. Here's an email she sent me before one of our sessions:

> Really looking forward to working with you tomorrow!
>
> Quickly checking in on where you'd like to work. Looks as if we've another scorchio day on our hands – at least until the thunderstorms arrive early evening. Are you still good for a session outdoors – or would you prefer the relative cool of parasolled garden shade or being at your desk? I'm happy with any of the three options – just let me know!
>
> If outdoors, I'll call you at 11.00 so we can connect and you can walk yourself into your question and the session. Choose somewhere that'll support you and your exploration. Saying factor 101 and a hat is SO teaching you to suck eggs!
>
> (Claire Sheldon, 2021)

It's a great example of managing contracting, weather, location and client preparation.

In Summary

Weather conditions are a great additional dimension to the coaching experience. One which mirrors the world we all live in. A component of life over which you have no control but which can have a significant impact. It's fascinating to experience what the weather can add to a coaching session. Just imagine the tranquillity that comes from a frosty sunny day with sharp clear air and a sprinkle of glitter everywhere – magical. I've yet to meet anyone that doesn't love them; just beware of it being icy underfoot!

In all the time I've been coaching outdoors, I've only ever moved one session inside due to poor weather, and that's not because we've toughed it out; it's because, more often than not, the weather is absolutely fine.

A reminder:

- Check the weather.
- Contact your coachee if there is any inclement weather.
- Contract around their comfort level.
- Is there any clothing/kit information that would support them?
- Plan the route/location accordingly.
- Have a quiet back-up space available in case the weather worsens.

 Activity – Your Weather Boundaries

Reflect on your comfort levels in various weather conditions – damp grey winter days, cold days, scorching hot summer days, blowing a hoolie days, showery days. Pick moments when you have experienced those – choosing one at a time, close your eyes and take yourself back there…

- Where were you?
- What weather elements were you aware of?
- How were you feeling?
- Was there anything specific that bothered you?
- What was the impact?
- Where was your attention focused?

This is an ongoing exploration. Keep investigating what weather you are comfortable in over the next year so that you know your boundaries in each weather condition.

Clothing and Kit

It seems to me that an understanding of the natural world is crucial for all of us – after all, we depend upon it for our food, for the air we breathe and, some would say, for our very sanity.

David Attenborough (2009)

WILL YOU TAKE a bag? A rucksack? A notepad? A pen? Should you wear jeans? A woolly hat? Will you take water for yourself and do you take one for the client? So many questions. In this chapter we take a look at clothing and kit. If you like executive summaries, you'll like this. There is no right or wrong; do what works for you and learn as you go.

Clothing

The main consideration for what you wear is that you make sure you are comfortable, so that you can give your full attention to your coachee. You don't want to be worrying about being too hot, too cold, having a blister, etc. So, first things first – what's your Achilles heel and how do you avoid it? I am always cold, so I wear plenty of layers. Even in summer you'll find me with layers on that I can easily remove and I love tops that zip all the way, as I can then pull the zip up for warmth or down for ventilation. My neck is always cold so for most of the year I have something that fits snugly around it – either a polo neck, a mid-layer that zips up quite high or a buff. As I shared in the 'Weather' chapter, I've also found that I don't like cold wind in my ears and that I get a headache if I get too cold, so I wear a hat in winter. I'm still on the hunt for the perfect hat – I've gone through a few!

It's so valuable to become clear on what will support you being comfortable. It's well worth taking the time to find out what's going to give you the best chance of being free of niggles and then have your full attention available to your client. If you are worried about sunburn or a blister then you are not going to be fully present.

A must for everyone is a good thermal. You can't beat them. Something that will keep you warm if you find yourself sitting with clients on a bench, and yet is breathable and works with your body temperature so that you don't overheat if you are moving. Merino wool is great. Another good staple is a polo shirt. They always look smart and can be added to in winter for warmth or worn on their own in the summer. Another summer consideration – beware of nettles and ticks! While shorts/skirts may be great in the sunshine, they do not lend themselves to protecting your legs. It's also a good idea to let your client know if you are walking somewhere with things that sting or bite, so that they can choose their clothing appropriately too. Each season presents different considerations and while we don't cover them all here, a bit of pre-thinking about the season, the weather and the route will help you plan for both clothing and kit.

Lastly on the clothing front, take a waterproof (or at least a 'shower proof'), because there will be days where you don't quite know what the weather is going to do – and it's good to be dry. If in doubt take a waterproof jacket. If you choose wisely, you'll only need one which can be worn all year round. A thin shell is best, then you can layer up underneath for warmth in the winter, or just wear it over a lightweight top in the summer. If it does rain, I have found a baseball cap hugely useful instead of putting my hood up. Hoods cover your ears, making it harder to hear your coachee, and they cut out your peripheral vision which makes things quite a bit harder when you are walking side by side. Baseball caps also have the added benefit of keeping rain off glasses. None of this has to be expensive. You probably already have appropriate things in your wardrobe; it's just a case of finding them and striking the right balance between professional and practical. Clearly an office suit and shoes would be impractical, while full hiking kit seems extreme and would probably scare your coachee!

Footwear

Rule number 1 – whatever is comfortable and preferably something with a bit of grip. Then consider your terrain – is it muddy? Is it wet? Is it both? Is the path uneven and stony? Do you get blisters? Do you have bad ankles?

And the weather: is it likely to rain? Is it frosty and therefore slippery? Do you suffer from cold feet? Has it been snowing? I once went plodding through ankle-deep snow with a client; it was amazing – we had the best session making footprints in virgin snow, surrounded by silence and sparkling white. We were both prepared for the snow and therefore took advantage of the glorious day. It would have been a very different experience if we'd been in trainers and jeans! I have two footwear mainstays: a pair of approach shoes which are like robust trainers and a pair of walking boots. Both are incredibly comfortable, grippy and waterproof (look for a Gore-Tex label). On hot summer days I wear light trainers.

It's also worthwhile considering socks; good-quality thick walking socks keep your feet warm in winter but do they fit in your shoes? And in the summer little socks are great, but I find that if they are too short, my shoes eat them and tiny stones flick into them too easily and then I'm forever stopping to pick them out. I know it seems like minutia but detail really is important when it comes to comfort.

Kit

Water: Will you feel better if you have a drink of water with you? Some people have a drink with them wherever they go. If this is you, then take water. Others would find that a water bottle gets in their way – then don't take one. Personally, I like one with a loop so that I can carry it easily, and an open neck so that I'm not sucking through a straw; taking ages and making a racket! Some days I take water, some days I don't.

If it's going to be a hot day and you have a water bottle then either mention it to your client beforehand or take one for them: '*Would you like one?*' is a thoughtful offer versus '*Here's some water for you*', which sounds a little bit more like an instruction.

Sunglasses: These present a little bit of a conundrum. Squinting into the sun is not a good look and gives me a headache, but having my eyes covered while coaching feels like I'm placing a barrier between us. When I wear them, they are invariably up and down like a yoyo! There is also the option of a baseball cap – it keeps the sun from your eyes (and showery rain from your glasses!) but can be seen, by some, as being quite informal. Once again, it's what works best for you.

Pen and Paper: The question that I am asked by coaches in every conversation I have about coaching outdoors is what I do about pen and paper when I'm on a walk. '*Tell me, how do you manage to recall what was discussed on a walk if you don't write anything down?*' – Colleague, October 2019. Here's my response: I trust that I have all the resources I need (NLP belief) to recall everything that is relevant from the session and once I'm back at my car I take a few moments to note down the salient points. It's never failed me yet. I have actually found that my recall is really good and that I not only recall the main facts, I am also more aware of my felt experience. In fact, my notes are better because they are less factual minutia and more my felt experience, patterns I noticed and client reactions. They include thoughts or observations, hypotheses and ideas for the next session. All round they are richer and more valuable. A colleague retraces the walk in his mind after a coaching session. He finds that the route walked provides anchor points for the conversation and he has a comfortable recall of the session for his notes.

So, what about the client? I have a little stash of small notebooks and small pens (both pocket size), which I take along for my clients if they want one. I talk about note taking in the contracting phase and offer to equip them if it's something they would usually do. Of all the coachees I have offered this to, two have taken it up. One of them writes in every session and we often stop for her to write things down. Mostly we stop to sit on a bench while she writes, but with a small, good-quality hardback notepad, it's also easy for her to write while standing. The other client has never used his notebook.

Sit Mat: It's great to have the option to take a seat with clients either on a bench, a log or on the ground. In perfect weather you'd just sit down but no one wants a soggy bottom from sitting on a damp log. So, I take a couple of sit mats along with me. I used to take plastic shopping bags but they're not very environmentally friendly and offer no insulation. A sit mat is very simply a small waterproof mat (think tiny camping mat/yoga mat) that folds up or rolls away, offering some insulation from the cold and protection from a damp surface.

Map: A map is not a necessity if you or your client are familiar with the location. If it is somewhere new to you both, often it's easy to take a look online or at the venue (parks or National Trust properties often have maps on display) and then take a snapshot on your phone. On a 60–90-minute session, you are unlikely to need more than this. If you are out coaching for half a day or more, or you feel that route finding has an important role to play in support of your client, then you will probably want to take a map and compass with you or have a map that can be accessed easily on your phone, if there is signal! Some map apps allow you to download the map. While there is no legal obligation to carry a map, it wouldn't be very professional to walk with a client and find yourselves lost or needing help and not to be able to get back or tell the emergency services where you are!

Bags: By this point you'll be unsurprised to read that sometimes I take a bag and sometimes I don't. Some of my colleagues do and some don't! If everything you want to take fits comfortably in your pockets, then great – no bag required. If it doesn't, then you'll need a bag. And again, no surprise, take the one you are most comfortable with. A waterproof bag is a good idea, as you can put it down anywhere and not worry about its soggy bottom or become distracted thinking about getting a wet phone if it rains. Rucksacks make an obvious choice and come in many sizes. They are practical, usually waterproof and very comfortable.

First Aid Kit: If I'm in an urban area and out for less than two hours, I do not carry a first aid kit. When I have been in wilder locations and out for longer, I always take one with me. Legalities may vary by country so it's best to check what is required in your area. My advice here is to do some research and give it some thought and make the choice that you are comfortable with.

Insurance and Training

With adults, on low-level walks in the UK, there is no need for you to be trained or insured. As far as I am aware, having dug around extensively (in UK law), there is no requirement for your insurance to be any different from the standard public liability insurance. I have let my insurance company know that I am working outdoors; it has had no impact on my policy. Working with children is different, so if this is your field, I strongly suggest researching the cover you need.

When I work with groups or individuals outdoors, providing we are not working at over 600 metres (2,000 feet) I do not take along a qualified instructor. However, when in higher terrain I work with a mountain guide. I have made my own judgement based on my experience, the group or individual's experience, the route and the conditions. All of that feeds into my risk assessment. Legally (UK), I do not need to have anyone qualified along but I would feel exposed if anything was to happen. Once again, it's very much down to personal comfort levels.

Please bear in mind that this information is, to the best of my knowledge, accurate and relevant at the date of publication. It's best to check what the current legislation is for your region before you make any plans beyond a stroll in the park.

If you have an interest in gaining some qualifications in leading outdoors or are looking for a guide to come with you then the recognised qualifications (in the UK) are shown in the diagram below.

LEADER TRAINING

LOWLAND LEADER

HILL & MOORLAND LEADER

MOUNTAIN LEADER

WINTER MOUNTAIN LEADER

INTERNATIONAL MOUNTAIN LEADER

A great place to find out more is www.mountain-training.org

Supporting Your Client with Their Choices

My Coaching Outdoors programme delegates often muse over the following: *'At the risk of being parental and controlling, should I tell my client what to*

*bring?' 'If I say nothing and I've got a waterproof/drink of water and they don't,
I'll feel awful.'* I approach this as though I'm having the conversation in an
indoor setting: *'I'm going to order a coffee, would you like one?'* or *'The air con
in this building makes it a little cool; I always bring a jumper'.* I wouldn't have
a second thought about saying either of those, so I take the same approach
to being outside. I include it in the pre-session contracting as part of my final
communication about session prep – *'Looks like there's a chance of rain, I'm
going to have a waterproof with me'* or *'It's looking windy, I'll have a hat on'.*

In conclusion, the key objective with all of this is that your clothing and kit
supports you in your work and doesn't get in the way. Each person's preferences and choices will be different.

A great book which supports this chapter well is *Hillwalking: The Official
Handbook of the Mountain Training Walking Schemes* by Steve Long.

Activity – Explore Location and Kit

A chance to explore a new coaching location (building a location
portfolio will make your work easier) and try out some clothing and
kit choices.

- Pick a place, look at the weather and decide what to wear and
  take.
- Go for your walk.
- What worked? What didn't?
- Did everything feel right?
- What changes, if any, would you make?
- What would you adapt for hot/cold/wet/windy weather?
- The section mentions Achilles heel: what's yours? How do you
  make sure you are not caught out/remain comfortable?
- What's your perspective on first aid kits and qualifications?

Give It a Go

So that's it. The end of Section III. We've covered a lot of ground already.

- We've set the scene.
- You know the health, wellbeing and cognitive benefits of walking outdoors.

And we've explored:

- Psychological safety considerations
- Contracting for success
- Location ideals
- How to manage the weather
- What to wear and take

 Activity – Have a Client Session Outdoors and Reflect on It

You are now very well equipped to have a coaching outdoors session with a coachee. So, to quote Nike, '**Just Do It**'.

… and afterwards make some time to reflect on how it went.

- What was your experience?
- If possible, explore your client's experience.
- What went well?
- Anything you'd change?
- Through the lens of each area we've covered so far, what did you notice?
- What is important for you to cement?
- Is there anything you'd do differently?

Section IV

Nature and You

Your Nature Connection

If you truly love nature, you will find beauty everywhere.

Vincent van Gogh, 1890

I'VE WRITTEN IN previous pages about the importance of the coach's connection with nature. About our comfort level and connection being as important as the client's. The coach in relation with nature is an incredibly important aspect of this work. Afterall, there are three participants in this collaboration: coach, coachee and nature. Having a strong and continually developing relationship with nature is fundamental. Being a great coach outdoors begins with your personal connection to the natural world. In this chapter I offer you an opportunity to consider what nature means to you and what your regular outdoor practice is.

Having your own relationship with nature and being in tune with it will support you effectively when collaborating with nature in your coaching. You'll have noticed that throughout the book there are as many activities for you as there are for your coaching practice. That is very much by design, giving you the stimulus to enhance your own nature practice and connection. It all starts with you!

The way you coach outdoors will be different from mine and anyone else's. You will demonstrate your passion in a different way; you'll favour different techniques and you'll have a different way of being in nature that is formed from your life experiences. The stories you tell about what the outdoors means to you and why you are drawn to it will also be unique. This is the chapter where you get to bring that from your sub-conscious to your consciousness. It is the foundation to your outdoor practice. It will help you connect with why you want to work outdoors beyond the previously highlighted benefits and how collaborating with nature fits with who you are. Just as the demand on today's executives is to be congruent in their leadership, so too is the requirement for the coach to be authentic in their work.

We're going to take a look at your historical relationship with nature and the meaning it has for you. To highlight what I mean I am sharing an excerpt from my MSc action research dissertation on 'How are we in nature and how does it shape the quality of our coaching conversations?' (Roberts, 2016, p.24). I'll then share the process with you so that you can explore your story.

> The reflection began with my earliest experiences of being outdoors and much to my surprise, it was not what I had found there; it was what was missing. I could not recall a time when I had been in the outdoors with my parents. I had no recollection of ever being at the beach as a child or going to the park etc. My earliest memories were of playing on my swing alone (again) in the back garden. As I explored further, up to university age, it became more and more apparent that although I loved the outdoors and got a lot from it, it began as a place that was mine, somewhere my parents did not go and crucially my mother was not there to criticise me or be confrontational. It was my place of sanctuary, freedom and daydreaming. A substitute parent perhaps? Totton proposes that 'If their childhood was difficult, they may well feel that their other-than-human carer protected them from despair' (2011, p.191). I now realise that this would have been a sub-conscious wish for my clients when we have worked outdoors. I hoped for my clients the same 'care and support' that nature offered me.
>
> I then considered what my outdoor experiences were as an adult. I explored my time at university, covering finding outdoor pursuits and majoring in Outdoor Education. I thought about my time in Inverness Hospital where, during a two-week stay as a result of a rock-climbing accident and facing the possible amputation of my lower leg, I'd got through the pain and remained positive. I never doubted that I'd be able to do sport again even though I was told it would be unlikely due to the severity of my injury. I believe it was in part due to my bed being next to a window with views out to the hills. Ulrich's research (1984) on hospital room views explains this in evolutionary terms: Natural environments trigger positive

emotional reactions because observing nature was once important for human survival.

Throughout all of this I discovered a pattern: In all the places that I had lived I'd recreated the childhood experience of my swing: Curbar Gap near Chesterfield, the flat rock next to the river in Applecross, Whale Warf in Bristol, a walk round the Harewood Estate, the bow of the boat on the Clipper Race, Rutland Water near Oakham. All places where I feel present, calm, relaxed and nourished. '*Time stops when I am outside, the pressures of life fall away; it's just me and the real world.*'

The meaning I made from this: I thoroughly enjoyed my 'walk down memory lane'. I was surprised at the discovery of a 'safe place away from my parents' and of how I had continually recreated that through my life. I was intrigued by the possibility of a substitute parent. Could it be that although nature is not linear, I feel no discomfort with that, and no desire to be in control of myself or others when I am outdoors, because I feel supported by nature in the way a child would by a 'nurturing parent' (Berne, 1964) as Totton (2011) suggests? Nature is a great resource for me in my life and a superb companion to be with in my coaching relationships.

Now it is your turn...

 Activity – Your Relationship with Nature

Pick a walk or location in nature that you love – it doesn't have to be wild. Somewhere you feel safe and inspired. An environment that supports your thinking and reflection.

Consider the following... (If you don't know or are unsure of any answers, walk a little and see what you are drawn to; how is that relevant to the question?)

- What was my earliest remembered positive outdoor experience?
  - What made it positive?
  - What about that was important to me?

...⟶

- What other significant experiences have I had with nature in my life?
- What has nature given me throughout my life?
- How is this part of who I am?
- What is my relationship with nature like?
- What do I now have in my life / what do I now do that is congruent with being outdoors?
- What does being in nature bring to my work?

This may be a series of walks that you take. There is no rush. Just see what evolves.

Your Nature Connection Practice

I go to nature every day for inspiration in the day's work.

Frank Lloyd Wright, 1959

WHAT ROUTINE PRACTICE do you have for spending time in nature? In this chapter we consider our own nature practice and its value in promoting our (re)connection, sense of belonging and wellbeing.

Here's a lovely example of finding support in nature from my colleague Caroline Hampson who takes daily morning walks:

> *I woke up feeling a tad grumpy with the world but watching mummy duck so proudly leading her ten little ducklings through the park brought a massive smile to my face. Nature has an amazing power to soothe.*

Caroline's story is just one example of how her daily walking commitment resourced her. Other examples of nature practices are:

- Walking daily in nature with silence, curiosity and wonder
- Taking your 'free child' outdoors
- Finding 'sit spots' that are inspiring and spending regular time there
- Marking important life events with more extended time outdoors
- When stuck, taking a well-formed question outside and seeing what comes

In essence, your nature practice is all about you. About taking time in nature to resource yourself in whatever way serves you well. Your nature habits. The closer we are to nature and the more connected we are with nature, the better we are going to be at collaborating with nature in our coaching practice. One way we can do this is to have a commitment to our nature practice.

My time in nature has varied wildly over the years from snatched moments on the parental school walk to spending a year at sea on a racing yacht crossing the world's oceans, and most things in between. My colleague Fi Macmillan's model 'The Nature Switch Continuum' is valuable in helping to recognise and categorise exactly what time we are spending in nature.

THE NATURE SWITCH CONTINUUM

Fi Macmillan 2020

I value this model because it has helped me to recognise that, due to having a full and busy life, I've been neglecting to find micro wild and wild time often enough for me. Each of us will be different and what we need to feel resourced will be different. I know that for me a moment in nature is beneficial, but a weekend outdoors feels like I've had an opportunity to recalibrate mentally and physically and connect with what really matters. And if I can have an extended period of 'wild time', it's like I've won the lottery!

Fi describes her outdoor practice as having three clear benefits: 1) Keeping her sane and happy. 2) Becoming more conscious of her somatic experiences, which in turn supports her coaching work. 3) Valuing the thinking space that is created for her when she steps outside with a question in mind.

Activity – Your Nature Switch Continuum

Take a look at the nature switch continuum.

- What activities do you have that would sit in each category?
- How much time do you spend in each category?
- How do you feel at each stage?
- What does that experience resource you with?
- What's the right balance for you?

As life changes and our needs shift, we may need to adjust what works for us. Perhaps increasing the frequency of the micro dose to compensate for less micro wild time or fuelling up on wild time and daily doses because micro wild becomes hard to obtain. The key, however, is to do it consciously and make sure you are getting what you need.

You'll notice that Fi's model is based on 'doing' and time spent being outside in the main. And, of course, that brings with it all the benefits for mind and body that I wrote about in the benefits section. However, there is also the practice of communing with Nature – taking time to appreciate, notice and learn from her. For example:

- Growing a plant
- Watching your cat/dog/fish
- Tasting freshly picked fruit or veg
- Marvelling at the intricacies of a snowflake
- Walking barefoot on the grass
- Feeling spongy, damp moss
- Listening to birdsong
- Looking up at an ink dark sky speckled with stars

More of a commune than a 'do'. Here's a great example of what a 'commune' with nature could offer you, from Wendell Berry's poem 'The Peace of Wild Things' (2012):

> *I come into the presence of still water.*
>
> *And I feel above me the day-blind stars*
>
> *waiting with their light. For a time*
>
> *I rest in the grace of the world, and am free.*

 Activity – Commune with Nature

Take a look at the above list of suggestions to commune with nature or explore your own.

- Choose one to commune with.
- Push away distractions.
- Give yourself the gift of 10 minutes.
- Spend your time being fully present and in relationship with that element of nature.
- Afterwards, take a moment to reflect; what happened for you?

The nature switch continuum and communing will contribute to an ever-evolving CPD journey with Nature as your teacher and support.

I'd like to leave you with Schultz's (2002) Inclusion of Nature in Self (INS) model. It was one of the first measures developed to assess nature connectedness (that I introduced in the 'Planet Benefits' chapter). It has been used countless times across diverse populations. It simply asks people: 'How interconnected are you with nature? Pick the diagram that best describes your relationship.'

INCLUSION OF NATURE IN SELF MODEL

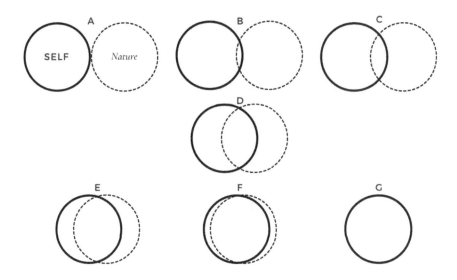

Perhaps you might like to consider: How interconnected with nature would you like to be? What will you do to achieve this?

Section V

Nature as a Co-Facilitator

What is Nature as a Co-Facilitator?

Nature has a wonderful power of putting things right, if allowed free play.

James Platt, 1883

THIS CHAPTER IS deliberately placed after the previous one. In my experience and evidenced in that of others, you are more capable of collaborating with nature as a co-facilitator if you have surfaced your relationship with nature and developed your own practice first. Here I explore the powerful role nature can play in the coaching relationship. I share some thoughts on collaborating with nature to unlock insight and awareness and share some stories of real-life examples. We begin by clarifying what it means for nature to be a co-facilitator.

Leary-Joyce (2014) points out that the quality of coaching is in the coach 'being' rather than the coach 'doing'. That's a brilliant piece of advice for coaches, and especially those who work outdoors, as by us 'being' we allow nature in to do some of the 'doing' – sharing in the relationship alongside us.

Consider the following from a *Guardian* article about forest schools by Liz Lightfoot (25 June 2019), quoting Helen Davenport, co-author of *Critical Issues in Forest Schools*:

> 'Being sat around a fire, being fully immersed in whittling a spoon… children building a shelter with tarpaulins, sticks and ropes or making face paint out of nettles and some making bracelets out of saplings. It's so calm. It's magical.'

On the other hand, she knows of sessions where what goes on inside is brought outside: 'I've seen written work from the classroom brought outside with worksheets and, on one occasion, desks as well,' she says. 'That is not forest school, nor is it when the children come out to find laminated posters stuck to trees with number challenges and marker pens.'

Totton (2014) has a theory that nature becomes a 'third party' in the relationship.

If we take a look at the 'Nature as Co-Facilitator Dynamic' figure in the 'What is Coaching Outdoors?' chapter, it is easy to see the relationship and the spectrum of working in depth with nature highlighted in the *Guardian* article above.

When outdoors, nature is truly an active participant in the coaching relationship. Partnering with nature as a co-facilitator is about consciously inviting nature in – all being in the relationship together. 'Addressing the environment not merely as a setting but as a partner in the process' (Berger, 2009, p.46). The experience of engaging with nature offers richness, depth, new perspectives and 'magic'. It can be as simple as offering a client a moment of reflection while looking at a beautiful view, allowing nature alone to positively support their meaningful reflection. Really skilful coaches step back almost entirely, allowing nature to do much of the coaching! '*Putting trust in nature to co-facilitate meant that I put less pressure on myself and gave more time and space to nature and the client*' – Heather Wright, Coach.

When we coach outdoors, at one end of the spectrum, it may just be taking the indoor conversation outside. In the middle, the coach invites nature into the coaching conversation, expanding the process and opening the door to additional dimensions, unlocking things which would likely not have been reached without nature's active presence. At the other end, the coach stepping back to a minor role allows greater dialogue between nature and client. Berger (2009) describes a triangular relationship between the therapist, client and nature. He details how direct sensory contact with natural elements can be a powerful stimulus for deeper thoughts and feelings. In particular, it can benefit clients who have difficulty with connecting to emotions or being able to express themselves (you can see an example of this in one of the vignettes in Section VI, p.165).

There are many conversations when we work outdoors. The human-to-human conversation is one but there are also more subtle conversations, ones with weather, plant-life, terrain, animals and other humans. There is an opportunity to be aware of the manner in which these are met, along with the associated conscious, unconscious and non-conscious meanings and experiences evoked.

(Marshall, 2016)

Nature is a living, sensual place, evoking work that involves all the senses and communication channels: physical, emotional, imaginative and spiritual (Abram, 1996; Roszak, 2001). Working with nature as a partner in coaching can be transformational for coach and client.

The multi-faceted world of 'we-in-context' relating (Tudor, 2011), if well 'caught' by the coach, can promote insight. Collaborating with nature as co-facilitator invites multi-dimensional awareness.

- What's happening in my client?
- What's happening between my client and nature?
- What's happening in me?
- What's happening between me and nature?
- What's happening between my client and me?
- What's happening around us (in nature)?
- And how are we jointly in relationship with nature?

The perspectives above represent opportunities for the coach to notice and then choose what to attend to.

 ## Suggestions for Framing

I'm often asked, '*how do I bring nature into the conversation without sounding a bit "tree huggy" or "weird"?*' I have found that offering what's there 'lightly' works well.

- I'm noticing this…
- My attention is drawn to that…
- Could that be significant?
- What's the difference for you standing in the shadow? The light? What's in your shadow?
- What are you noticing?
- In what way is that relevant?

Again, it's about trusting your intuition on whether you want to bring your observations into the conversation. Nothing ventured…

Here's a simple example – a moment of collaboration with nature from one of my client sessions. We are in a setting that is familiar to both of us. The coachee has been talking about a difficult situation where she is struggling to make headway.

Just as I ask, '*How long can you continue in this way?*' we arrive at a clearing with views over the water. We are walking companionably side by side, slowing as we reach a junction. To our left is a path bordered by fields that takes us to a bench at the water's edge; to the right the path continues into the woods. I ask JP, '*Which path would you like to take?*' I am aware that I'm talking about the route ahead and her metaphorical path. JP chooses the path to the seat with the view. She remarks how lovely it is to find somewhere new in an area that is familiar to her; she has not been down this way before and appreciates the expansive view. I ask her, '*In what way is that relevant?*'

I felt as though there were three of us in that coaching session. When nature participated in the session, we were offered a real-time experience to draw on.

Working with clients… outdoors changes the didactic nature of the work, because there is now a third party involved… the other-than-human occupies the third apex of a triangular relationship which also includes the client and therapist. Sometimes it facilitates the relationship between the two humans, for example by commenting on something that has been said with birdsong, a crack of timber, a quick shower, or a gust of wind.

(Totton, 2014, p.16)

 ## Suggested Exercises – Transference

A last offer in this chapter of how you could co-facilitate with nature. I cover many more ideas in the following chapters. Buber (1923) suggests that as soon as we see something we are in relationship with it. We project our own emotions onto it. Therefore, the natural world provides a safe and neutral canvas on which we can see our inner landscape and, if we wish, project our feelings onto. Transference would be one example of how we could use this with our coaching clients:

Example 1

- Pick something that represents X (boss, partner, mother, etc.).
- What sense do you make of the thing you have chosen?
- If that tree/stone/sheep/duck was your boss, what would you say to them?
- Now what do you notice?

Example 2

- What would your life be like if you were not carrying X?
- Pick up a stone, push into it all that you want to remove from your life; a feeling, a situation, a thought, a sensation.
- Say something about it.
- Would you like to throw it into the water?
- Now what do you notice?

In Summary

Trust Nature to be your co-partner. Allow her to be the inspiration. Find your way; what tools and techniques are you comfortable with? What works for you and your clients? You'll know through practice, trial and error. Chris Holland, an outdoor learning educator, has a lovely phrase for the relational dynamic, 'Nature does the teaching and we adults are the classroom assistants!' (2014, p.18).

Activity – Your Current Practice

Consider your coaching outdoors work currently.

- Where on the line are you in terms of collaborating with nature as a co-facilitator?
- Where would you like to be?
- What steps will you take to get there?

NATURE AS CO-FACILITATOR DYNAMIC

Taking the indoor conversation outside

Stepping back and allowing nature to be the coach

Lesley Roberts 2020

Metaphor and Mirror

The richness I achieve comes from Nature, the source of my inspiration.

Claude Monet, 1926

Metaphor

THERE ARE MANY opportunities for clients to explore aspects of the natural world that match and illuminate their internal experience. In this chapter we look at metaphor and mirror. I demonstrate how we can work with what nature offers our clients, building on the principle from the previous chapter of the coach stepping back and letting or inviting nature in. I begin with a stroll through the value of metaphors in coaching, including sharing some examples and offering some exercises for you to use with your clients. I also explore signs that nature offers us, mirroring and constellations with stories and suggested exercises.

The word metaphor comes from the Greek *metapherein*, which means '*to transfer*'. In communication we use metaphor to transfer meaning from one thing to create awareness or understanding in another context. Metaphors are rich sources in helping us build greater understanding of something. For example, 'he stormed out of the room' conveys greater richness than just 'he left the room', and opens up an opportunity for exploration through many avenues. Coaches and clients find metaphor incredibly valuable in surfacing understanding that is beyond conscious knowing. Metaphor opens up avenues of expressing things we find difficult to put into words: emotions, experiences, jumbled thoughts or desires. Professor of linguistics Zoltán Kövecses has shown that four out of six of the most-used sources of metaphor are in the living and physical worlds. So intrinsically we are drawing on our natural world connection to help us better understand.

'The natural setting can of course, be a canvas on which to project and an opportunity to work with metaphor' (Marshall, 2016). When coaching with nature we might ask: '*What do you see that represents X?*' Visual metaphors are a short code that engage unconscious and complex understanding that sits beyond words and cognitive function. Metaphor is deeply personal so it's a treasure hunt for the client to find what's meaningful for them.

> Metaphor is abundant in the outdoors… the space offers a language for people that don't necessarily know how to put words to their feelings… In a place full of metaphor, you can see what they're drawn to and say '*[in what way] is that relevant?*'
>
> (Dr Ruth Allen, *Ramblings*, 12 March 2020)

 This is a story from a client I have worked with for over a year. We are in the same outdoor location we always walk in.

NG wanted to explore his style of leadership, saying he didn't know what type of leader he was. I invited him to look around us at all the trees, both near and far, and to pick one that he was drawn to. I then asked him to describe what he saw when he looked at the tree.

'It's next to the water, standing alone from the other larger trees but near some little trees.'

'And what else?'

'It's enjoying the view, being able to see all around.'

'Anything else?'

'It's providing shelter for the smaller trees.'

'And in what way does that relate to your leadership?'

'I'm not with the crowd of other leaders. I'm standing alone, a bit different. I like to stay connected to the people that are coming up, to help and support them. That interests me far more than all the politics and meetings of senior leaders. It's the people beneath me that are important.'

NG kept being drawn back to the tree metaphor. The conversation expanded from him as a leader to the system (the landscape around) and the challenges he might face (fierce sun, hard frost, flooding). We have been able to come back to this tree as an anchor moment. It gives us a short cut to that moment and a rich language. We've also visited the tree through the seasons and considered whether what the tree is experiencing at the time is mirrored in NG's present experience.

Had the setting been different I might have asked NG to choose something else: a cow, a plant, a bird. Here are some other metaphor examples which your location may offer.

Bridges

- *The bridge from what to what?*
- *The bridge between what and what?*

Stepping stones

- *What are the first steps to X?*
- *What small steps can you take?*

Sunrise/sunset

- *What is dawning for you right now?*
- *What would you like to put to bed?*

Wind

- *What cobwebs would you like to blow away?*
- *What needs a refresh?*

Woodland

- *In what way does the woodland system represent your organisational experience?*
- *What's it like stepping into/out of the shadow/shade of the woodland?*

Egg shell

- *What new beginning are you experiencing?*
- *What are you emerging from?*

Our opportunity as coaches is to observe and catch these metaphor gifts when they present themselves and integrate them into our work. Knowing when they add value and insight and when they might be a distraction or not resonate is a bit of a skill, but with practice it gets easier and if it doesn't go quite right then we learn from it. It's well worth it. Here's a reflection from a client of mine: '*Using metaphors in nature as a trigger for thinking about things differently particularly resonated and helped bring out deeper issues and self-understanding*' – Jayne Chidgey-Clark. And a recounted experience from a Coaching Outdoors programme alumni coach and her client:

> *They found themselves being struck by metaphors nature offered and using them to express what was present for them 'outside of my head'. It moved the coachee from cognitively thinking it through in the same old way. It offered something different, refreshing and exciting.* – Sheryl Clowes, Coach

And finally, here's an example of the value working with metaphor can have for both coach and client.

> *As part of working with a client on living his values we discussed 'towards vs away moves' – daily reflections on whether his actions/behaviours had moved him towards living his values or away from them. I invited him to choose something from our surroundings that represented these. For 'towards' he chose a beautiful old oak tree – solid and grounded, yet still growing and developing. His 'away' was a sign (of the 'do not walk on the grass' type). He shared his hatred of bureaucracy, process and people who say 'can't do it'. This metaphor gave me an insight into how he liked to work that I don't think I'd have otherwise been aware of (and I ensured I kept our coaching support processes light touch after this!).* – Sam Eddleston, Coach

Examples of Enquiring Metaphor Questions

Choose something that represents:

- How you are feeling
- This situation
- Your relationship to X
- How big the problem is
- The problem
- You now
- Where you want to be
- What's important to you
- The way forwards

 Suggested Metaphor Exercises

Check In – Check Out

Here's a simple exercise from my colleague Sam Eddleston. Ask a client at the beginning of a session to pick something from the surroundings that represents how they are currently feeling, e.g. clouds scudding across the sky representing being under pressure and moving at pace. Then check back in at the end of the session with the same question. It is interesting to see any shifts that have been made.

Representation

Ask your client to select something (tree, duck, sheep, flower, etc.) that represents someone or something. Then explore the thing they have chosen. '*Describe what it is about X that is reflective of Y*', '*In what way does the roughness/warmth/vibrancy/strength of X relate to Y?*', '*In what way does that impact you?*'

Signs

Sometimes nature offers us a sign, a message. We may or may not mention these to the client. The following examples help me to explain this concept.

The Owl – It was 3 o'clock in the afternoon and I was sitting on a bench with a client while she was reflecting. I could hear an owl in the background. I was weighing up whether or not there was some benefit in acknowledging the owl to my client; after all, it is unusual for an owl to be awake at 3pm! Or should I leave it? Given the moment and the context I decide to leave it. In my reflection notes I mused over the owl, '*what was the significance?*' I was curious. The next time I was with the client I asked her '*Are you getting a good night's sleep?*' '*No I'm not; I'm awake through the night with things just going on in my mind.*' We then explored this. Her lack of sleep may not have come up had I not asked the question based on my owl noticing and reflections. Perhaps nature had a message for us? Perhaps a happy coincidence?

The Yellow Bird – Sitting on a bench with a client exploring where his feeling of guilt came from. He was sitting in silence as he did not have an initial conscious answer to the question. A little yellow bird (yellowhammer I think) appeared in the long grass just in front of us. It was well camouflaged and I'm not sure if my client saw it or not. To me the little bird represented the client's mother. I'm not sure why or where the idea came from. Shortly afterwards he began speaking about his mother and his feelings of duty and their relation to the situation he was currently carrying some guilt about.

Different Views – An experience I had just last week that I shared with my client, where nature offered me a mirror to what might be happening. I was walking with a client through a patch of woodland next to the water's edge. The client was talking about the impact that their line manager's behaviour was having on them (fear of poor performance). I had a hunch that they were reading into the situation something that wasn't there but wasn't sure whether to offer it or not as I didn't want to appear dismissive of their feelings and I could well have been wrong. Walking side by side, I was enjoying the view out over the water. I knew that AD was looking at the woodland with its dappled shade and carpet of bluebells. I became aware that the experience we were having mirrored my intuition – there being more than one view and him not having that perspective. The experience reinforced my hunch and emboldened me to offer '*Let's stop a moment, there's something I'd like to show you*'. We talked about the two views and he shared that he hadn't considered an alternative reason for his line manager's behaviour. He left the session committing to holding a conversation with his manager to explore his recent decisions and behaviours.

I wonder how many people have had similar experiences and how many are reading this thinking, '*well, it's just a coincidence*'? I'd like to think that you might consider: '*what if nature really is offering us something?*'

Mirror/Parallel Process

Many of you will be familiar with the term *parallel process* (Searles, 1955), involving the psychoanalytic concept of transference and countertransference. Transference occurs when the client recreates the presenting problem and emotions with the coach (or coach with supervisor), while countertransference occurs when the coach responds to the client in the same manner that the client responds to the originating situation. Thus, the coaching relationship replays, or is parallel with, the activating event. Initially Searles referred to this as 'reflecting'. Sometimes nature offers us a mirror/reflection to something we are experiencing or talking about. Unlike seeking out a metaphor, where we may have invited the client to find something that is 'as' or 'like' something else, where the stimulus has come from the coach, often a mirror experience comes along unprompted by the coach. Here are a few examples.

> Coach Claire Burgum recalls an outdoor phone coaching session between her and her client.
>
> It was a winter morning and I began the session without much of a view due to the mist hanging over the river. Towards the end of our conversation, I found myself back at the same spot on the river bank. I was asking my client about her insights from the session when I found myself looking at a beautiful view in glorious sunshine. I shared with her what I was seeing. The perfect clarity now the mist had lifted, which chimed with her getting clarity from our conversation. A beautiful connection with nature that I was seeing and she was feeling.

Remember Richard from the 'Weather' chapter and our wet, grey, elemental walk at Curbar Edge, where he was comfortable in less inclement weather?

> The weather that day served as a mirror for Richard's current work experience. He was having a tough time at work with a number of challenges but knew there would be light at the end of the tunnel. He said he just had to 'manage through' his current situation. He was aware of the impact on him and was still within his window of tolerance (Siegel, 1999; Ogden, et al., 2006). He knew it was not sustainable long term and said that his comfort with the current adversity was due to his previous experiences and knowledge and the fact he knew it was only going to be short-lived.

Coach Sam Clarke found that paths often appear as a powerful reflection of choices.

> I noticed this well-trodden path in the field and recognised how well this supported the conversation my client and I were having. We were talking about limiting beliefs and how we have often reinforced them over time, until the belief is a habitual way of thinking and becomes our truth. Looking at this path, it appeared that this was

the chosen way to cross this woodland and our default was almost to follow it simply because it was well-trodden. Yet we can choose a different path if we want, a different belief, and open up a whole new experience for ourselves. I shared this with my client then gave her the choice of how we crossed the woodland.

The following is taken from the podcast series *A New Earth*, in an interview between Oprah Winfrey and Eckhart Tolle (2014). Tolle says:

> When I was writing 'The Power of Now' I took a break to sit in a park on a bench by a pond. I saw two ducks approaching each other; suddenly they got into a fight. It lasted 30 seconds or so and then they separated and swam off in opposite directions, still agitated. They lifted themselves up off the water and vigorously flapped their wings a few times then were totally peaceful again. I realised I had been writing about this [the human species and managing negative emotions]. The ducks were showing me how they let go of what otherwise would have become accumulated negativity in the body. Their instinctive natural intelligence takes over. After a fight the energy gets dissipated through wing clearing. [Most humans are not as good at managing emotions.]

In this story we not only see the reflection of what Tolle was writing about but nature adding value by demonstrating a better way to manage state.

Elements of nature can also be a mirror of the internal emotional or cerebral landscape. A picture creates a thousand words. Once created, the image can be used by coach and client to jointly explore what they see before them. You could also invite them to photograph their creation.

 Suggested Mirror Exercises

Map

Use natural things to create a map or picture of:

- events;
- the problem;
- the challenge;
- the issue;

- desired outcome;
- how you feel.

Learning tree

At the end of a session, ask '*Can you see the wise oak over there? Imagine it's been listening to our conversation so far, heard all of it.*'

- What has it noticed?
- What would it say?
- What advice would it give you?

Becoming Open

Connecting with all the opportunities described in this chapter has been an evolution for me. With practice I have become more attuned to what nature is offering. We can practise becoming open to connecting with mirror, metaphor and signs on our own walks, allowing nature to be our coach each time we step outside (free coaching, what a gift!). Here's an example from coach Toni Smerdon's LinkedIn post from 2020:

> Just allowing my mind to drift as I walked back from shopping I noticed these blackberries, all at different stages of ripeness. It led me, in that moment, to reflect on how everyone (myself included) is currently at a different stage in their journey through coronavirus.

And my own walk.

> I saw a silver birch yesterday on my walk; it was heavily bent over but had grown most of its branches on one side to counter-balance the bend. It made me reflect on how I am adapting in these current times to manage life's challenges. I was also struck by the fact that the tree had silent grace and that was in stark comparison to how some people manage challenges. I reflected on whether or not I had the same silent grace when times are tough.

From my colleague Sam Clarke, 2020:

> I decided to put pen and paper down to do some kingfisher spotting, having seen them before in this very spot. I was gazing in anticipation for around half an hour but the beautiful birds were elusive today. I started to wonder if perhaps I was trying too hard and that

beautiful things often happen when I just let go… And as I lowered my head to capture this thought, the unmistakable flash of turquoise passed by, just 10 feet in front of me, gliding low and slow over the water, as if it had been waiting to show me… OK, message received!

Constellations

Constellations were initially used to explore family dynamics but have since become a tool that coaches work with to map and explore the system clients are part of and how things relate to each other within that system. The methodology reveals previously hidden information which can then free up movement for something new to emerge. Rather than dive into the process of constellations here – it could be a whole chapter in itself! – I'd just like to take the opportunity to highlight that if you feel a constellation exercise would support a client's insight, it is possible to create a rich constellation through the use of natural resources: a woodland, the landscape in front of you, a flower bed or by gathering relevant objects and placing them in front of you. A point to note is that this work is surely named after the star constellations!

Suggested Constellation Questions

- What drew you to X to represent Y?
- What do you notice?
- If you were to place yourself here, where would you be?
- And others?
- How is that?
- What do you see?
- What's that like?
- How would you like it to be?
- What position would you like to have?
- What happens when you view it from a different perspective?

The bounty of resources available in the natural world offers vast richness to both coach and client in the ways of helping explanation and unlocking insight and understanding. It is well worth becoming attuned to what nature is offering you and then deciding what to do with what is offered. I have never found that offering a metaphor, mirror or constellation causes a rupture in the relationship; often, they offer a 'lightbulb' moment or deep understanding of something previously unexplainable.

 Activity – What is Nature Offering You?

Take a relaxing walk.

- What did you notice?
- What was nature offering you as a mirror, metaphor or sign?
- What will you do with the insight?

Rhythm and Seasons

I like to think that to one in sympathy with nature,
each season, in turn, seems the loveliest.

Mark Twain (1835–1910)

THIS CHAPTER IS packed with information and ideas on how we can actively engage with nature's rhythm and seasons. We begin by looking at the concept of time and then I write about each season in turn, offering a vignette, suggested coaching questions and an activity for each.

Nature's Rhythm

Life on Earth is shaped by nature's rhythm: the Earth's daily spin causing sunrise and sunset, the Moon cycling through a month impacting our tides, the Earth orbiting the sun creating our seasons. Plants and animals show profound daily and annual cycles in response to environmental cues yet, in the main, the Western human population seems oblivious. In our modern, fast-paced and technology-led world we have become separated from nature; we have lost touch with the daily, monthly and seasonal variations of our natural environment. Our built environment with access to heating, electricity and imported foods, especially year-round seasonal fruits and vegetables, has enabled us to maintain the longer days and eating habits that we would normally only experience in summer. Living in this way we have become disconnected from the lessons, opportunities and impact of nature's rhythm. We live in an age of technology that is advancing faster than we can keep up with. We are part of nature and therefore experience relaxation when we step outside and join with nature's rhythm because it is our own.

'Time stops when I am outside, the pressures of life fall away; it's just me and the real world' – coaching client.

Our modern lifestyle also impacts our sense of time. In the capitalist-driven world, time is of immense importance to us. We set time for things, allocate specific amounts of time to jobs, measure time with clocks and calendars, and think of time as linear. *Chronos* time (that which is measured by the clock) is very important to us. *Kairos* means 'time', but a different sort of time to Chronos. Kairos is mystical time, moment-to-moment time, time where the action suits the context. This kind of relationship with time is supportive for a person to enquire, to explore, to learn. It is also nurturing for both coach and client. Let's explore further.

Kairos is an Ancient Greek term meaning a fleeting opportunity that needs to be grasped before it passes; not an abstract measure of time passing (*Chronos*), but of time ready to be seized, an expression of timeliness. Just think of a child at play; they are in Kairos time, fully present and engaged in what they are doing with no sense of Chronos time. Young children have yet to be 'conditioned' to Chronos time; they don't understand why they have to hurry up and get ready for school, to leave the house on time, whereas a frustrated parent is worried about their child being late for the 9am start. The child is far more connected to the natural world where things change when they are ready.

Seasons

Consider the gradual seasonal shift. It occurs when all the elements are just right; only then do trees' leaves begin to turn in autumn or blossom appears in spring. Reconnecting with the seasons brings us back to a long-lost appreciation of doing things at the opportune time. Chronos is about quantity; Kairos about quality and the now. Being seasonally aware and in tune with nature invites us to be more 'in the now', following the rhythm of the natural world and benefitting from the opportunities nature presents. We have become divorced from the natural world, from spring's bright green hope, summer's abundance of life, autumn's colourful slowdown and winter's fresh stillness – the natural cycles and timings of the Earth.

We are nature. We have seasons in our lives too and by connecting more to nature's rhythms we can support ourselves better. The simple need to conserve energy and hibernate in winter. The desire to lean into the feelings of growth and newness in spring. To use the energy of the summer to make progress. And the shift of being grateful and then letting go in the autumn ready to embrace the next change. We can work with the 'seasons as a framework for how we live our lives, to create balance, rhythm, and awareness, and to live our lives with connection, joy, and intentionality' (Cluett, 2020). The same is true in coaching. The seasons reflect the duration of the relationship. And a client may feel that they are in a particular season, either in their life, in relation to their time with an organisation or person, or how they feel about a situation. Each situation mentioned is an opportunity for the coach to bring a seasonal frame to the coaching conversation should they choose to do so.

ATTRIBUTES OF EACH SEASON

The season of preparation
Sowing seeds
Increasing energy levels

The season for action
Energy levels are high

The season of rest
and reflection
Low energy levels

The season of harvesting
Letting go and preparing for rest
Decreasing energy levels

Lesley Roberts 2020

Each season has a different flavour, a different energy and is part of a wholistic cycle. Let's look at each in turn, along with an idea of how you and your coaching clients can connect with the seasons.

Spring

Spring is nature's way of saying 'Let's Party'.
Robin Williams, 2014

Spring is a time of emergence. Perennial plants and deciduous trees grow new leaves, annual plants germinate and grow, some plants blossom, hibernating animals re-emerge and, for others, this is the birthing season. We are surrounded by signs of new life. We can use this new beginning to plan, explore, learn and begin to take action. I'm a big believer in saving 'new year's resolutions' for spring. There's a much greater chance of being successful when starting something new with the energy of spring than there is in the depths of winter! Spring is most definitely nature's 'new year'.

What follows is an example of working remotely with nature in an intervention between coaching sessions.

My client was stuck, unable to take action. She was feeling a sense of inertia. I had been working with her for over a year; it was unusual for her to be feeling this way.

'Isn't it about the right time to be planting this year's tomatoes, cucumbers and peas?' I asked.

'Yes, I haven't even touched the greenhouse yet,' replied my client.

'A bit like those work projects then?' I commented.

Laughing. 'Yep, seems I've no motivation for planting either.'

'OK, I've also not tackled my greenhouse. Fancy a challenge?' I offered.

'You know I like to win, don't you?!' she said with a twinkle.

'Yes, I do. Let's see whose tomatoes have grown most by our next coaching session. I'll send you photos of how mine are getting on and you can send me your more impressive ones,' I laughed.

By the next time we met her tomatoes had indeed grown more than mine (fortunately!). While she had not gained any traction on the work projects, the tomatoes were doing well and she had planted her cucumbers too. We explored how she felt about the progress she was making in the veggie growing and what was different between that and the work projects there was inertia with. It turned out that, unlike growing tomatoes, which she saw as something very simple to do, the projects were complex and she felt unsure of where to start and what to do next. We began to explore this more by building a picture of how she had learnt to grow vegetables for the first time and what levers she had used for support.

 ## Suggested Spring Coaching Questions

- What seeds will you sow?
- What has begun to grow that needs attention?
- What possibilities are there?
- Who do you need to connect with?
- What action do you need to take to meet your goals for this year?

 ### Activity – Dawn Chorus

Spring is a great time to hear the dawn chorus. In spring, before the sun rises, male birds declare their presence in a bid to attract passing females. Their music concert grows as the sun comes up. Perhaps just once in the year you could get up early, before the sun rises, and bathe in the sound of the day coming alive as the sun comes up and a new day dawns. 'The psychological effect of being in the dark before dawn and then hearing the chorus swell as the sun comes up is just incomparable' (McGeeney, 2016, p.6). Early May is a good time; any later and you'll be up in the middle of the night and some birds sing less once they have a mate!

Summer

Live in the sunshine, swim in the sea, drink in the wild air.

Ralph Waldo Emerson (1803–1882)

Summer is the season of growth, vibrancy, abundance and brightness. Plants and animals are highly productive. Plants invest in growth and create fruit. Animals also focus on growth and on helping their young to become more self-sufficient. The natural world is full of colour and warmth.

We can use this energy for action. Create, build, develop, network, etc. during this period of high energy and outward focus.

Here's a lovely example of a summer coaching experience from my colleague Sam Clarke.

It was an early evening coaching session; D was sitting in his garden whilst we talked. Once he was settled, I asked him if he'd like to take a moment to take a few breaths and just 'Be'. He said yes.

'Think I needed that,' he said.

'What's happening?' I asked.

'Well, I clearly need to get out more for a start,' he said. He went on to explain a situation at work, a colleague to whom he needs to give some challenging feedback but he's been putting it off. *'I'm just feeling completely stuck with this,'* he said.

'OK, take a breath again and focus on being in the garden, D. What do you notice?'

'There are loads of bees and butterflies,' he said.

'What do you notice about them?' I asked.

'They're very busy, moving from flower to flower. And weed to weed actually! I can't believe how many weeds there are! Another job to do,' he said.

'What happens if you don't get the weeds out?' I asked.

'Well, they're just going to multiply and probably strangle some of the strawberry plants,' he said.

'What will help you?' I asked.

'Well, it will be better if I get them out before they get too big; I just need to get on and do it and remind myself of the benefit,' he said.

'And what benefit will you get when you do it?' I asked.

'I'll feel better for some time in the garden and the plants will be able to thrive and produce more fruit,' he said.

'Do you think nature may be offering you a way forward?' I posed.

Suggested Summer Coaching Questions

- What is blooming in your life right now?
- What have you been putting off that needs attention?
- Where will you place your energy?
- What action do you need to take?

 Activity – Feel Nature

Summer is a great time to take your clothes off! As the temperature rises, we begin to shed our layers. With longer, warmer days comes a sense of freedom and lightness. Nature invites us to walk barefoot on the grass, sit on a log for a picnic and paddle in the sea. So come on, take those shoes and socks off and feel the cool grass under your feet or the soft sand between your toes. If you're feeling adventurous then perhaps the freedom and exhilaration of swimming outdoors, allowing the water to reinvigorate you as you glide along.

Autumn

Notice that autumn is more the season of the soul than of nature.

Friedrich Nietzsche (1844–1900)

Autumn is the season to prepare for winter. As the nights become longer, plants' fruits ripen and drop and animals may hoard food or further increase their consumption in preparation for winter. Trees begin to rest and draw down sap. They release their leaves to the ground, which become shelter for animals and eventually nutrients for the soil.

We can use this time to refine what we have produced in our summer and enjoy our harvest. It's also a chance to let go of things that no longer serve us.

An example of the coach bringing the season's offering into the conversation. Session 1 with this client.

My client and I had been walking through a country park when she observed that there were a lot of acorns around this year. We briefly mused over what created a 'mast' year. And joked about there being many happy squirrels. Later in the walk my client mentioned:

'I am overwhelmed with work and pulled in so many directions, both work and home. The problem is I don't want to give any of it up; it's all good stuff and really valuable.'

I am reminded of our acorn observation and say, *'The situation reminds me of all the acorns we saw earlier, so many of them, all valuable and full of goodness.'*

'Yes, it's just like that. I don't want to let any of them go. There's value in all of it. But I can't do it all at once.'

I think of the 'happy squirrels' eating some acorns and hiding some for later. I ask, *'If you were a squirrel, would it be possible for you to "squirrel" some of the things away for later?'*

From here we had a fruitful (pardon the pun) conversation about how she could manage the overwhelm and still do everything, just not all at once.

In my experience of working outdoors with clients it is not uncommon for such wonderful coincidences to occur. It's a pleasure to become really attuned to what Nature is offering and to work with her. The bravery comes in trusting what you notice and offering it lightly to your client and seeing what they make of it. In the vignette above it felt completely natural to make the link and to offer it to my client.

 Suggested Autumn Coaching Questions

- What can you harvest and celebrate from your hard work so far this year?
- What do you need to let go of?

- What can you 'squirrel' away for later?
- What preparation do you need to make for the next quarter?

 Activity – Berries and Leaves

Autumn is a great time to taste nature's bounty. Taking an autumn stroll to pick blackberries from a hedgerow, enjoying a few as a snack (have at least one in a mindful way if you can!) before 'squirrelling' the rest away for an apple and blackberry pie. Even if you don't have a garden, it's hard to go far in the UK without coming across a blackberry bush with its tempting juicy dark fruit. And of course, whose 'free child' (Berne, 1964) can resist kicking a pile of leaves and watching their golden colours drift down through the air. Or listening to their crunch as you crush them on your walk. Autumn is a rich season in all senses. Just taking a walk outside away from central heating and screens is rewarding and invigorating in itself.

Winter

To appreciate the beauty of a snowflake, it is necessary to stand out in the cold.

Aristotle (384–322BC)

As the nights grow longer and the cold seeps in, winter is an opportunity for rest. The deciduous trees become completely skeletal, seeds often overwinter in the soil, and certain animals hibernate. Much of nature 'sleeps'. There seems to be a stillness about the land.

We can use this opportunity to rest and reflect. To restore ourselves from the year that's gone and fuel ourselves for the year to come. View the clarity of the empty landscape and consider what clarity we need or have for the year ahead.

This is a great example of nature as co-facilitator during a coaching session in the winter. I had worked with this client for three previous sessions.

We'd had a lot of snowfall, but the sun was shining. I wondered if my client would still want to walk and if he had appropriate footwear; it transpired the answer to both was yes so off we set. The snow was deep; it was more plod than walk! We were in a rural location with not another human soul and virgin snow all round us. There was a magical sense to the day and a feeling of freshness.

In two previous sessions my client and I had been 'tip-toeing' round the topic of his relationship with his father and how that impacted the man he was today.

'My dad used to work really long hours and was never around much but one winter when we were kids, I remember him taking us sledging; I think it was a Sunday but it was still unusual for him not to be working.'

I enquired what the experience had been like for my client to have that time with his dad.

'It was great, I loved it, it was one of the few times I remember him spending time with us and not telling me off.'

'Telling you off?'

'Yeah, he was always telling me to try harder.'

In the first 15 minutes of our walk, I knew more about my client's relationship with his father than I had discovered in any previous session. That magical winter's walk was an 'unlocker' for my client being able to share and explore his relationship with his father and what that might mean for him now.

The conversation arose naturally. As the coach I was not putting in the work; nature had offered an opportunity/catalyst and my client had accepted the invite. It's one of the simplest examples I can think of where nature not only co-facilitated the session but led it; all I had to do was make sure I didn't get in the way!

Suggested Winter Coaching Questions

- What do you need to do to rest?
- What will nurture you through the winter?
- What are you grateful for this year?
- What are your goals for next year?

 Activity – Nature's Soap Opera

The empty landscape of winter means there is less food around for the animals who haven't hibernated. If you'd like to spread a little festive kindness, take some seeds or oats to the ducks and watch their feeding time behaviours. Observe how they fight and bully each other for the food and yet when it's all over hold no apparent resentment, nor do they try to get revenge! Explore how different species react to the food and to each other. It's a natural soap opera getting to know individuals through firstly their appearance and then their personality.

The Senses

In each activity above of how we can connect our senses with the season, there is an opportunity to offer those moments in coaching. Invite someone to walk barefoot, smell a plant, listen to an animal, mindfully eat a blackberry. *'My coachee felt they had a real penny-dropping moment through the power of exploring outside and the use of senses'* – Amanda Nelson, Coach. You are inviting them to engage with the world around them and relate to it, stimulating their senses and encouraging them to think and experience differently. What is common across all five senses is that they literally reconnect us with our bodies. By engaging somatically, you are also opening the possibility of easier access to emotions, memories, feelings and creativity. In these moments there is the possibility of helping someone become unstuck, inspired or enlightened by inviting them to consider: *'What do you notice?'*; *'In what way does this experience relate to X?*'; '*What is this experience offering you?*' Connecting with our senses is also a way of reducing anxiety in that moment. When we pay attention to our senses, we shift our focus and become present, moving away temporarily from what is causing us to feel anxious.

Of course, you could also suggest your client takes time before your session for the seasons connection activity and then jointly enquire into their experience and how it relates to your work together.

Knowing Yourself

It is also worth giving some consideration to the fact that you and your clients may not experience the seasons in the same way as would be typical. How do you feel each season? Do you notice that you have more/less energy in summer? While summer generally is associated with energy, you may find heat oppressive or have medical conditions exacerbated by heat; therefore, autumn may be when you 'blossom'. How are you in winter? Do the cold, short, damp days depress you, or are you a lover of a cold walk in quiet woods, a crackling fire and the chance to rest on dark evenings? What are the implications of this for you? Both in terms of self-care and a possible mis-match in needs and output from others? Is there anything you need to do to attend to this? I pose these questions as food for thought for you but also as possible questions for your clients.

Bringing the Seasons Inside

An opportunity to continue the connection to the seasons when we are in our homes and offices is to bring something of the season indoors. Many of us do this unconsciously in winter when we have a fir tree in the house, which we decorate for Christmas. Often, we have holly, mistletoe and ivy too! Think of Halloween, those pumpkins and spiders' webs (yes, autumn is the time of giant spiders in the bath; that's because the males increase their movement in a bid to find a mate!). It could also be an opportunity to place some shiny conkers on your desk, some dried grasses in a vase. What about some crocuses or hyacinths on the windowsill in spring? Or some collected shells and driftwood placed in a bowl from a summer beach walk? Not only are these nice to look at and resource us in a way a computer screen never could, they can also be anchors for our seasonal experiences.

In Summary

The seasons offer more richness, vibrancy and opportunity than you'll ever find in any coaching model or tool – a bounty of opportunity just waiting to be engaged with.

Activity – A Sensual Seasonal Walk

A sensual, seasonal walk. Give it a go yourself. You could also offer it to a client either as part of a coaching session or as pre-work.

Set some time aside to take a relaxed meander in nature, connecting fully with all your senses.

- What do you notice?
- What are you seeing/hearing/smelling/tasting/feeling?
    - For example, in autumn you may smell woodsmoke, see the warm autumn colours, notice squirrels scurrying to collect nuts, hear the crunch of leaves and the crack of twigs under-foot, feel peaceful as leaves drift down around you or in awe at the colour transformation, taste the blackberries and feel the smoothness of the conkers.
- Just take it all in.
- Immerse yourself in it.
- Allow yourself to be fully present.
- Listen with your heart, body and soul.
- Then, later, notice what you notice; what comes up for you?

Trust Your Intuition and Give It a Go

Fortune favours the brave.

Latin proverb

S o that's it. The end of Section V all about nature as a co-facilitator. In Section IV we dived into your relationship with nature. And in this section we've explored mirror, metaphor and seasons.

Now it's time to put it all into practice with a client. It is at this point that you are probably wondering about the balance of when to bring nature into the conversation and when not to. How to work with all this richness in a way that is natural and not 'clunky' or 'forced'. It's the most common question I'm asked at this stage. '*How do I get the balance right?*' Once again, you'll be very familiar with my answer – each conversation is different. There's no right or wrong. Sometimes you may make a lot of nature references; sometimes, very few. It depends on the client, the day, how you are feeling, what nature offers, etc. Trust your intuition. I've referenced intuition a number of times through this book. In a bid to equip you a little, I'd like to share some thoughts on intuitive knowing and what's to be gained/lost by trusting our intuition or not.

Intuition

Intuition comes from a place deep inside. Intuition is intelligence of the unconscious kind – the intelligence innate in nature. Intuition is independent of instruction but not of experience. A way of knowing that we are unable to rationally evidence. It's a hunch, a thought, a feeling, relating to the situation we find ourselves in. Scholars (Hodgkinson et al., 2009; Salas et al., 2010; St. Pierre & Smith, 2014) propose that 'professionals could – and should – tap into quick-fire intuitive intelligence' (Sheldon, 2018, p.7). Sheldon's research on 'working at the boundary' captures four ways of working with intuition and maps the impact of these interventions on the coaching relationship.

WORKING WITH INTUITION

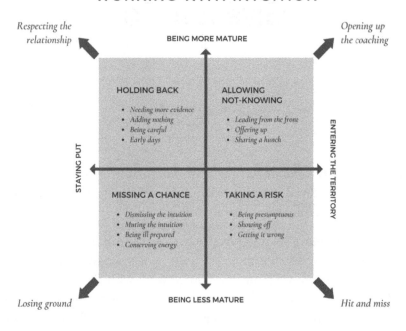

Claire Sheldon 2017

From her work we can see what happens when we 'lightly' offer something (top right) we are intuitively noticing or thinking. Erik de Haan (2008) notes that coaches make intuitive choices all the time about what interventions to use in coaching and that it is part of what makes us individually unique. Collaborating with nature is no different. Just as you would in your normal coaching practice, trust your hunches, gut instinct and judgement and do what 'feels' right for you. There's only one way to develop and that's to give it a go and review what the impact is.

Activity – Go with the Flow

Let's do this. Take a coaching client outside and put some of your new insight and ideas into practice. Be prepared to go with the flow.

After the session reflect on:

- How was it?
- What happened?
- What did nature offer?
- What, if any, great questions or exercises did you use?
- What did they bring up for your client?
- What went well?
- What do you now know?
- What will do you next time?

Section VI

Teams and Working Remotely

Working with Groups and Teams Outdoors

Nature does not hurry, yet everything is accomplished.

Lao Tzu, 6th century BC

ONE OF THE questions I am often asked by participants on my Coaching Outdoors programme is: *'Please can you talk about the coaching work you have done with groups and teams outdoors?'* Therefore, it feels important to include that insight in this book.

I have worked with teams of 4 to 24 and from green spaces in city centres to the wilds of Scotland, from young offenders to CEO teams. The principles are the same. In this chapter I share considerations, experiences, client feedback and stories. The main focus of this chapter came directly from a Coaching Outdoors programme participant's question: *'What are the key differences between working with teams and working with individuals in an outdoor space? How do you manage the psychological safety etc. if you have a challenge with one member of the group but you have multiple people with you?'*

The Difference Between Groups and Teams

Let's begin by considering and defining the difference between group and team coaching, before we move the context to an outdoor setting. A good example of a group is of a collection of people who have gathered in the same place for a similar reason, such as attending a training or development programme. They are unlikely to know each other and may well never see each other again. A team, on the other hand, most definitely do know each other and will see each other regularly. Teams are usually found in organisational settings. They have to work collaboratively to reach an outcome and if we are talking about a high-performing team, they'll be inter-dependent in pursuit and delivery of their purpose.

From here on I refer to 'team' but it could just as easily be a group.

Contracting and Psychological Safety for Teams Outdoors

As we did with individual clients, we need to start with contracting for working with teams outdoors. There is a need to consider the increased number of 'moving parts', just as there is with indoor teams. Within the team, you will have multiple tolerance levels for terrain, distance and weather. As I highlighted in the 'Psychological Safety' chapter earlier in the book, there is the risk of some things being triggers for people and as there is more than one person with you, then the risk is greater. Therefore, contracting is critical. I have a one-to-one conversation with each participant beforehand covering the ground mentioned in the 'Contracting' chapter. Then, considering the overall objective and desired outcome, I choose the location and design the session.

Chris Holland, a bushcraft teacher and nature lover who provides activities and support to parents, teachers and forest school leaders, takes a great approach to this topic:

> One of the guidelines by which I try to live is to work with Nature, not against... I try to read the nature of the group I am working with so that I can be effective. I have noticed that each group has its own feeling or 'field' and within it is a mixture of needs from the individuals. 'Reading' the group and fine planning has sometimes to be done on the hoof, occasionally the best-laid plans have to change. There are many challenges and huge rewards from working with nature... Any learning experience works best if the students have their enthusiasm awakened, before their attention is focused.
>
> (Holland, 2014, p.12)

Picking up on Chris's last point, to ease teams into the work outdoors I find a way to connect them to the venue and location in some form of pre-work. When we arrive, I create time for them to explore the location for themselves before we formally begin.

Location Choice

Quite a bit of location choice will be driven by practicalities: Where is each attendee geographically based and how far are they prepared to travel? How long does the event last? You don't want to be travelling to the Scottish wilderness from London for a day's team event! What's the right container for the desired outcome and where the team is 'at' (see the chapter on psychological safety for support on location choice)? What accommodation is appropriate and available? Once all that's been established, I make a few recommendations and we jointly agree where will be best. I love team coaching and have had the privilege to work with some great teams in a huge variety of locations from cottages in the Cotswolds, the Peaks and the Lake District, to bunk-barns and youth hostels in Devon, Wales and Scotland.

Nature as a Co-Facilitator with Teams

I have sat and walked with teams in fields, in forests, on beaches and up hills. We've worked and reflected together, in groups, pairs and individually with beautiful views. Every time, I have felt Nature partner with all of us, creating a resourceful space for the work. Her co-facilitation skills come even more to the fore with groups, especially when some individual or pair conversations develop at a different pace from others. Nature holds the space while everyone reaches the same place. There's always a view to be had, water to reflect beside, a tree or plant to marvel at. Nature holds the group together by creating a subtle thread of connection. There's no email distraction, nipping out of the room for a phone conversation or chat about the latest business figures or burning issues over coffee while waiting for others to finish. People stay much more present, respectful, connected to each other. I have also found that being outdoors with teams 'allows me to feel free to change my position within (or outside) the therapeutic space without jeopardising its maintenance' (Berger, 2007, p.44). This has brought me freedom to review the group's progress, attend to individual needs, reflect on my impact and consider what next at various stages. It genuinely is like having two coaches for the team.

Reflections from Participants

The members of teams I have worked with outdoors say that their feelings of psychological safety go up when they are in nature. When I asked why this is they have replied: *'Because we weren't in the office with all the "corporate bull-sh*t" and because I saw a different side to X* and *'Everyone was more relaxed and our perspective shifted because we were more connected with what really matters'*.

Neil Reynolds's (Mars Inc) experience was of *'A real "level set" and way to remove any remnant of hierarchy or formality. And the opportunity to offer upwards feedback in a less formal way as we walked and talked together.'*

Ben Thompson, a leader whose team I worked with in Scotland, said: *'Getting outdoors with Lesley allowed me and my team time to connect on a different level; more human, more honest, more vulnerable. Relationships were built and strengthened.'*

Eddie Johnson, MD UK, Ireland & Nordics, Keter:

> *Taking people and teams out of their normal environment no doubt creates an open mindset for learning and development, being out in the natural environment stimulates all of your sensors and I believe stimulates people to think much broader and out of their usual paradigms.*

And finally, from Isaac Fischer, MD, Pukka Pies:

> *We needed to have honest and open conversations on capability, reliability and intimacy. In my opinion being outside walking and talking in pairs really facilitated individuals' confidence for having tougher, braver conversations. I also feel it helped build their intimacy. The team came away from our two-day session stronger and with a new energy. I firmly believe being in an outdoor setting was pretty pivotal in that.*

Suggested Team Activities

Here are three vignettes from very different group experiences. Each brings coaching outdoors with groups and teams to life. They also highlight exercises that you could use with your clients.

 In this first story I was a coachee participating in a high-performance team event led by a coach. It was being run by an external facilitator (Chris). We were at a campsite in Bath and staying in teepees. The objective of our time together was to begin our journey to high performance. Specifically, we were focusing on our team purpose and building trusting relationships.

> Partway through the morning, Chris began to focus on team purpose. He asked us each to take a solo walk in the woods and fields and bring back something that we felt represented the purpose of the team. Off we went for our 20-minute explore.
>
> On returning we sat in a circle near the teepee and talked about our find, saying how it related to what we saw as the team's purpose. Chris captured key words we mentioned on a large piece of paper.
>
> When we'd finished, we placed all the objects in the middle of the circle. Chris asked us what we saw and again noted down key words from our descriptions.
>
> Collectively we then looked at what key words and themes had emerged from the exercise and reflected on what we saw, no judgements.
>
> Chris invited us to begin crafting our purpose statement. After about 15 minutes things became a little 'sticky' so we rolled up our piece of paper and headed off for a group walk with no other agenda than to find a lunch spot for our picnic.
>
> After lunch we revisited our purpose statement and somehow it just fell into place. The movement, break from it and change of venue seemed to have resourced us to 'see the wood for the trees!'

This second example is from my time working with youth at risk in Applecross, a remote location on the west coast of Scotland. You could use this technique with groups, teams or individuals.

After hours and hours of travelling across the UK, the groups would arrive at Inverness station for us to collect them and begin their two-hour journey to the centre. The last part of the journey takes a winding single-track road through the mountains of the Applecross peninsula and over the highest point, the 'Bealach na Bà'. When we got to the top we stopped the bus and asked the group to get out and stand on top of the mountain looking out over the sea to the Cullins of Skye. It's a powerful and awe-inspiring view.

We said: '*This is the start of your journey. You can choose to take responsibility and maximise every opportunity offered. To achieve, and commit to positive change. It is your journey to shape as you wish. You'll get out what you put in.*'

Back in the bus with many a grump and tired person wondering why on earth they'd been made to get out in the cold/wind/rain/midge-infested evening (this is Scotland, after all!) and on to their three weeks of personal development in the Scottish wilderness.

At the end of the three weeks, on the return journey, we stopped the bus again at the same spot. This time to invite the group to reflect on their experience. We gave some prompts: '*What are you proud of? What has been your biggest learning? What have you realised you are capable of? What are you committing to?*'

We also spoke about them having gained the self-sufficiency and tools to continue the journey without us.

The programme we ran had an 86% success rate of the young people not reoffending!

In my final story, I'd like to share with you some work I did with a corporate team. This was the first time I'd worked with this group outdoors. We were in rural Devon together.

> I'd planned an orientation walk through some woods to a clearing in a meadow.
>
> Along the way I asked the group to pick up an object that they were drawn to which represented how they were feeling about life at the moment.
>
> Once we arrived at the meadow, we sat in a circle sharing their objects as part of a check-in exercise. Each showing their object and saying something about it.
>
> The depth of what they shared varied. With those more surface-level responses or factual descriptions of the object, I asked simple coaching questions: *'And in what way does that relate to your life at the moment?'*; *'What is it about that, that's important you?'*; *'How do you feel about that?'* Each time using my intuitive judgement on how far to dive.
>
> Afterwards people in the team shared with me *'there's no way X would have said that if we'd been in the office'. 'I'm surprised by how comfortable I felt sharing what I did; I've not told any of the team before.' 'Wow, there's so much more going on with people than I'd realised.' 'I hope X is OK, I'd no idea.'* To which I replied, *'you could ask him if he's OK'.*
>
> I firmly believe we could not have achieved the same depth of connection and transparency had we been indoors.

Another great team activity outdoors is an evening campfire chat. I have found so much is shared in the dark round a fire. I suspect there is something about the setting and particularly the dark and the flames that draws things out as people share while looking into the fire.

In Summary

Working outdoors with a group or team is well worth the extra planning and contracting. How can you expect high performance from a day spent in an office? And nothing beats what you learn sitting round a campfire in the dark!

Remote Coaching with Nature

Study nature, love nature, stay close to nature. It will never fail you.

Frank Lloyd Wright, 1959

COVID-19 HAS BEEN a big springboard to the virtual world for many. It is definitely a more accepted way of working now. As a result, the geographical horizon of coaches' work has broadened. I have clients all over the world and just because I am based in the UK and my client is based in Africa does not mean nature can't join us in our work together. I know one coach who lives on a narrowboat and has his phone coaching conversations while sitting on a folding chair on deck, watching a huge willow tree swaying gently over the water in the marina. Introducing nature to our remote conversations can be a tonic to yet another virtual meeting. In this chapter we explore a number of ways to integrate nature into your practice when you cannot be together outside. We begin by looking at how nature can be brought into telephone coaching conversations. Then I suggest some really simple methods for incorporating nature into virtual coaching sessions and how you can bring nature from outside to inside to support you (and your clients) in your home office. I then share thoughts on outdoor virtual sessions before offering some little gems on nature connections between coaching sessions, finishing with an activity inviting you to get in touch and share your ideas.

The Good Old-Fashioned Phone

In my opinion, having a phone coaching conversation is the next best option to being outside with a client.

Firstly, let's take a look at getting the nuts and bolts right. Just as you would before any coaching engagement, you need to make sure you contract for the specific context you will be working in – in this case over the phone outdoors. Advise your client to pick a location away from traffic noise (it's quite remarkable how loud a car sounds down the phone). Also, ensure you both choose routes where you know the phone signal will hold and agree what you will do if it drops out. Make sure your phones are charged and have a back-up plan for what you will do if it is raining (phones and head-phones don't really like the rain). If it is incredibly windy (see car noise above) you might want to try a hat (in cooler weather!) to ensure you can hear and place your hand over the microphone to shield it from the wind. My colleague Clare Burgum does both and finds it still works well to be out in the wind. And finally, put in place the very simple agreement of who will call who.

Being on the phone releases us from the shackles of our laptops and frees our mind as well as our eyes to enjoy the world around us. Here's the phone coaching experience of one of my clients. It demonstrates the multiple bene-fits being on the phone had for her:

> *Covid lockdowns meant spending a lot of time in front of computer screens for meetings. Usually on camera, and, as a director, constantly being on edge managing facial expressions and voice tone to instil confi-dence throughout the team. With limited time for reflection in the day-to-day and screen fatigue, it was a relief to be able to step away from the computer and bring my phone out for a walk. Speaking with Lesley surrounded by our local park meant a thorough change in environ-ment and focus. It felt like me-time rather than being pulled in multiple directions by the needs and wants of others.* – Tanja Groth, SWECO

And another perspective from a second client:

> *It allows me to focus 100% on what is being said. I actually think my listening skills are now better on the phone after two years of Zoom – I can concentrate way better – not having to multi-task! Plus, I can enjoy nature – even on a walk just around Wandsworth Common – so I feel I am getting mental and physical stimulation too. We are all too station-ary – I struggle to do my 10k steps a day when working from home; this way I can get a lovely walk in and talk/be coached – good for the soul and the brain.* – Nic Waller, John Lewis & Partners

Pretty hard to argue with really and I experience similar benefits. I love being able to relax and focus on the client without worrying what my face is giving away as they stare at me through their laptop screen. I know from my reflections that my coaching work is better and that I'm a braver coach when I'm in person or on the phone. However, let's not get into all that. Let's take a look at what useful things I can share with you regarding nature and phone coaching. Whether you are inside on the phone looking out the window, both sitting in your respective gardens or both walking in locations close to your home, there are some great ways to engage with nature.

When I begin a phone session, I always invite my client to connect with where they are and to share that with me. We either have a quick 'Zoom hello', share a photo of our location or describe what we are seeing. These brief moments help me to feel connected to the nature in the client's space. It also serves to orientate them to connect with what is around them.

 One client I have enjoys working in her garden; each time we talk she describes what she can see:

I'm sitting on the bench under the apple tree. To my left I have the weeping willow that we planted quite close to the house, never expecting it to grow so tall. To my right I can see down to our orchard. In front of me is a bed with small shrubs; in the middle of it is a stone buddha, sitting very calmly surrounded by four stone balls at each corner. The sun is shining and it's just lovely to be out. The cat has also just wandered past and I can hear the neighbour's dog.

During our conversation when my client was describing a situation she was finding stressful, I recalled the buddha. I shared, '*I feel as though you'd rather be like your buddha than feeling how you currently do.*'

'*Oh yes, he sits there serenely knowing that "all things will pass". "This too will pass"; I need to keep reminding myself of that,*' she said.

I offered: '*Your buddha has four balls around him. If you were he, what resourceful things would those four balls be for you, things that are going to support you while you wait for this situation to pass?*'

This led to her describing four key things in her life that she can draw on to resource her.

Once again, nature was such a valuable partner in the work. My client had shared such a rich description at the start of our conversation that there were many elements which may have related to our conversation. I don't set out to use what is shared, but sometimes something from the initial description, something I am seeing, or the client mentions in the course of the call, offers itself.

As with other coaching outdoors work, you don't have to make reference to nature at all. We've seen from the client quotes above how much benefit being on the phone already brings and that's without nature being mentioned in the coaching conversation. It's your choice.

One thing that is important to mention – I still hold my chemistry sessions virtually. As I mentioned previously at the start of the chapter, visual clues are so important for building rapport. I have tried holding chemistry sessions over the phone and it has not worked anywhere near as well for me or the client. A concrete measure of this has been the number of clients selecting me as their coach decreasing when I held the chemistry sessions over the phone and going back up when I changed back to virtual. There's also the experience that I have of how well connected to the client I feel, which followed the same pattern.

Indoor Virtual Sessions (e.g. Zoom)

As I mentioned at the beginning of the chapter, the number of coaching sessions held over Microsoft Teams, Zoom and similar digital platforms has grown hugely from a tiny base since the outbreak of Covid-19. I know I am not alone in the fact that it was very rare for me to sit at my computer for a coaching session before Covid. It's now an almost daily occurrence and the last time I met anyone in an office for a coaching session was 4 March 2020. If, like me, some of your coaching is held virtually, do not despair; you can bring nature to these sessions too.

 Three Exercise Suggestions

1. I run a visualisation session at the start of group coaching video calls. I invite the participants to get comfortable in their seats, take three deep breaths and take themselves to their favourite place in nature. Using language that assumes they are there I ask them: '*What are you hearing?*'; '*What can you see?*'; '*With your hands or feet, what can you touch? How does it feel?*'; '*What can you smell?*'; '*Is there a taste to this place? What is it?*' I then say we are going to leave that wonderful place and come back to the session, inviting them to take three more deep breaths before they open their eyes and reconnect with the group. On return, we then discuss how the exercise made them feel or ask them to share their place with the group.

Doing a nature visualisation and senses connection at the start of coaching sessions creates a very different 'state' for people than the one they usually arrive with. It allows clients to mentally shift from their office environment to '*one where I am less connected to the "corporate system"*' – HD, coaching client, 2022.

2. One of the participants from the Nature as Co-Facilitator programme I run has created a reel of natural images and music that she plays for her clients when they are unsure of an answer to something or are stuck. She invites them to say which image they are drawn to with regard to the topic in hand and then they use the image to generate insight and possibilities.

3. This is the simplest of all. Invite your client to take a break from the screen and look out the window (standing up and walking

over to it if required). This is a favourite exercise of Peter Hawkins. Here are his follow-up questions: *'What grabs your attention?'* *'What do you notice?'*

By taking a break from the computer we change state, change the distance of our eye gaze, thus relaxing our eyes and giving ourselves a moment's relief from looking intensely at human faces. It's amazing how tiring staring at a screen can be and just a few moments looking away can make a huge difference. That's before you bring in the added value of connecting with the natural world and the insight a couple of questions can generate.

Creating a Natural Environment Inside

Just because you are working inside does not mean your environment has to be devoid of nature. My study has numerous elements of nature in it: plants, shells, pictures, pebbles and a seasonally scented candle. I'm also lucky enough to have a view out of my window over green space and with some glorious trees. When the weather is warm enough, I open the window to hear the birds and feel connected to the world. One client I worked with had conkers on her desk: *'they are relaxing to touch and remind me of the kids'* – Suzanne Coulton. Another has a beach rock: *'I pick it up and stroke it for a long time when I am feeling anxious'* – NP. Consider what will work best for you. Can you find a way to bring nature to all your senses in your office? And possibly have some things visible for your clients to see when they meet with you virtually – a plant in the background perhaps, a landscape picture on the wall.

Three Types of Outdoor Virtual Sessions

I notice that I've left this style of remote coaching session until last. It is because it is my least preferred method of holding a session. That's definitely a preference as I know it works for others. Let's explore three different types of outdoor virtual meetings. We'll begin with some considerations to do with tech! Now, I'm going to be honest here; as this is not my preferred way of working, I pose a few more problems than answers in the tech department! To be successful outside you will need to have a solution to the following: background noise, the client being able to hear you – perhaps a lapel microphone, lighting in winter, battery power, internet signal strength, a stable place for your laptop or iPad. Phones are too small unless you are right next to them. You're probably getting a sense that I'm not keen! It goes back to the principle of fitting my own oxygen mask first. I need to be at my best to serve the client and I'm definitely not when I'm outside with tech! However, let's have a look at people who are.

Nature as a silent partner – my colleague Simon Hawtrey-Woore has a 100% outdoor practice; the woods are his office. When he works virtually with a client, nature is the backdrop to the conversation; not an active participant for the client, but more of a silent partner for Simon. He always sets up a 'station' for the meeting and does not walk while on these calls. His clients, more often than not, are indoors. He has solved all the tech challenges and it works really well for him. He also wraps up warmly in winter and has a tarp for sun or rain protection.

Being outdoors with groups – my colleague Fi Macmillan has discovered that being outdoors and running a virtual session does work well with groups who are indoors. She has a unique setup where she places her laptop on a ladder, has a separate microphone and invites the group to connect with what they can see around her. This format brings her natural environment into their office.

In both examples, Fi and Simon are their best selves in these environments and therefore offering their clients the best of them. Your exploration will be to find out what works best for you.

The third type of session is having a virtual meeting while both yourself and your client are outside in different locations. So far, both myself and anyone that I have spoken to who has tried to co-facilitate with nature in a one-to-one virtual session with both coach and client on a screen outside has found it very distracting. The technology has got in the way of the benefits of being outdoors for both parties. Neither coach nor client are able to connect with the nature around them because they are still focused on the screen. One option that does work is to begin virtually, showing each other your locations, and then move to the phone allowing the other senses to connect with nature. Especially provide the opportunity for the benefits previously mentioned on 'soft fascination' (Kaplan & Kaplan, 1989), which are denied to us when looking at a screen.

Nature Connection Between Sessions

Many coaches will connect with their clients between the formal sessions, whether that's a touchpoint between sessions, a priming suggestion before a session or a follow-up post session. Here are some ways you can incorporate nature into this element of your practice.

 Priming Between Sessions

Let's start with a technique that you can offer to every client, whether you are seeing them face to face or working remotely. With a little bit of planning ahead your client can enjoy the benefits and insights that nature offers in between sessions.

Here are three exercises that you could offer:

1. An intention walk – invite your client to take a walk in a place that they find calming and resourcing. It might be a local park, the beach, on a dog walk through the woods or while they are gardening. While on their walk they hold in mind the following: *'What is it that would be most valuable for me to work with my coach on?'*

2. Repeat the walk above but with a different question. The invite this time is to notice what images or metaphors they are drawn to and then to bring them to the next session for you to explore. For example, you might ask: *'What was it that drew you to X?' 'In what way is that relevant to you right now?' 'What would you like to do with that insight?'* I am sure you have many of your own thoughts on great questions.

3. Walk as above, but this time your client brings back an object that represents their issue/how they are feeling/what they'd like to explore in your session together. And again, you would use simple coaching questions: *'Tell me about X', 'What properties does X have?', 'In what way is X representative of you?'* and so on.

Aside from the insights they have gained, my clients have found that the invite to walk before our sessions has given them 'permission' to leave their computers and created a catalyst for movement. From the coach perspective, those sessions have been very rich, both because the client is really ready and because we have accessed a different way of knowing.

 Suggested Touchpoints

Finally, the last way that I have found nature can be supportive in the coaching relationship when not together is through touchpoints between sessions. Here are some simple suggestions:

- Send your coachee a nature poem/quote to read before your call.
- Start your session 15 minutes earlier and both take a walk outside round the garden/street.
- Share a nature video clip to use as a bit of stimulus.
- Record a short video clip of you outside in a natural setting and send your client a relevant message.
- While I am on a walk, if I think of something or notice something that may be of value for a client, then I make a short video (sometimes with me in it, sometimes not, depending on the topic or if I'm looking presentable!) and send it to them on WhatsApp. It takes just a few moments with my phone held out and I know that clients appreciate it so much more than an email.

 Activity – Share Your Ideas

Tap into your creativity and explore what selection of methods works for you and your clients. Can you add something to my suggestions? If so, please let me know by emailing info@coachingoutdoors.com I'd love to hear what you've come up with and what the impact was.

Section VII

The Future

The Future of Coaching

I BEGAN THIS book in 2019 with no idea what was to come. When I wrote about the future of coaching, there were predictions that 50% of the workforce were likely to see some remote working by 2020; therefore, it stood to reason that the number of face-to-face and office-based coaching sessions would decrease and be replaced predominantly by virtual sessions. I thought that coaching outdoors would organically grow and because it was linked to wellbeing and growing from a small base that it would grow ahead of the curve. Well, the Covid-19 global pandemic and climate crisis accelerated all that. In this chapter I share my perspective on the key themes for the future of executive coaching and coaching outdoors.

Growth of the Market

The coaching industry is one of the fastest-growing sectors in the world, second only to IT (ICF, 2020), predicted to be worth $20 billion globally by 2022. And it's not just coaches who are coaching; many organisations now expect line managers and HR managers to be adept at coaching as part of their capability in people development. In a 2019 coaching study undertaken by PwC for the ICF, it was found that line managers and leaders who are coaching has risen by 46% compared to their 2016 survey.

Also driving the growth is the expectation that in business, leaders will be authentic and have high emotional intelligence. Therefore, the demand for coaching to support leaders developing self-awareness increases in line with his. It is also becoming common practice in large corporate organisations to include coaching as a standard part of leadership development programmes.

The future for the coaching profession looks very positive and filled with opportunity.

Accreditation and Regulation

As a relatively new field, coaching has survived thus far without a globally recognised standard for accreditation or regulation; anyone can call themselves a coach! However, with both the growth in the industry and the increasing number of coaches, that will not last for much longer.

Some organisations are beginning to make headway; the ICF (International Coaching Federation) and the EMCC (European Mentoring and Coaching Council) are becoming more recognised both by coaches and stakeholders. It is not unusual now for 'savvy' organisations buying coaching to be looking for coaches to have the ICF or EMCC accreditation. The 'quality stamp' demonstrates the coach's capability, experience, supervision attendance, professional ethics and commitment to continued personal development. And as demand increases and organisations create approved supplier lists, accreditation will be a key criterion for being selected. It's an easy way to initially help them 'sift the wheat from the chaff'.

Numerous coaches too want recognition for their many hours of CPD and coaching time. They want to be affiliated with professional bodies which lend credence to their profession and their skill set. Ten years ago, very few coaches or aspiring coaches asked me about my qualifications or affiliations; today, I am asked roughly once a month. When I reply that I have an MSc from Ashridge Business School in Executive Coaching, the follow-up question is usually, '*was it worth it?*' My answer is most definitely a yes, both in winning work and in my development as a coach. It's becoming clear that over the next few years it will be increasingly difficult to work in the corporate sector without recognised accreditation.

As for accreditation and legislation in coaching outdoors specifically, it is too early to tell, but my guess is that health and safety, risk assessments and insurance cover will play a part further down the line.

Corporate Experience

Along with organisations looking for people with recognised qualifications, they are also requesting coaches to have a business background, ideally at a leadership level or above. Stakeholders want coaches to have business experience and acumen; not just to have coached at a senior level, but to actually have held a senior position in a recognised organisation. Someone that understands the demands placed on the employees first hand. So corporate experience becomes another selection criteria for stakeholders when they are looking to recruit coaches; it helps to narrow down the field a step further.

The Need for Return on Investment (ROI) Evaluation

Return on investment used to be the holy grail in coaching and indeed all learning interventions. Until recently, that is. In the last three years not once have I had anyone ask me about measurement. I am not alone; colleagues also say that stakeholders now seem to believe in the benefit of coaching. They know there is no magic formula for measurement and are accepting of the value coaching brings without the need for statistical proof. I only see this belief in the benefit continuing and that, as the selection criteria for coaches become more stringent, the need for ROI will further decline.

Virtual Coaching

So much for the gradual increase of people working remotely! Covid-19 accelerated the virtual world for everyone, of which coaching was no exception. Coaches 'increased their use of audio-visual platforms (83%) [compared to 2016]' (ICF, 2021). And while it is likely that there will be a swing back the other way, the fact remains that virtual coaching as part of the norm is here to stay. I believe that while telephone coaching did not see such a huge rise (26%) compared to the situation in 2016, we'll see that figure increasing as people push back against virtual meetings. The telephone offers the same accessibility, safety and efficiency as the screen but with a chance to visually rest and physically move if we want to. In the next few years, coaches will have some clients that they only ever work with virtually. Other client–coach relationships will be a blend of virtual, phone and face to face.

Coaching virtually removes geographical barriers for coaches and clients, opening up a world of opportunities for everyone. It is therefore likely, over time, that coaches will build a portfolio of clients from a wider geography.

Coaching Specialisms

Whether it be in focus area or format, both coaches and executives are beginning to define what exactly it is they offer/want. When the executive coaching industry began circa 20 years ago, it was enough to be a coach/have a coach. As the coaching industry has evolved, so too has the working world and the demands placed on executives. Clients now want coaches who are specialists in specific areas: transition, menopause, resilience, female leaders, c-suite, group focused, strengths-based, outdoors, etc. And coaches are often asked '*what's your niche?*' Again, it's another way of meeting the needs of the business world today but also of narrowing down the choice of coach. This trend is set to continue for the foreseeable future – generic out and specialism in.

Future Proof

- Ensure you are accredited by a recognised provider.
- Find your specialism.
- If you want to work in business and don't have first-hand industry experience, find a mentor who will collaborate with you.

The Future of Coaching Outdoors

I've SEEN AN explosion of interest in this area over the last two years, massively accelerated by the impending climate disaster and Covid-19. In 2019, there were a handful of coaches talking about the work they were doing outdoors and encouraging others into this space. Fast forward to 2022 and there are coaches facilitating discussion forums, Ted Talks, articles being written, research being started, coach training programmes exploring the inclusion of coaching outdoors in their offering, and numerous posts on LinkedIn about the benefits and experiences of coaching outdoors.

As the pressures continue to grow on us in a demanding world, so does the need for wellbeing, quick wins and climate action. I believe that nature therapy will play an increasingly important role in both preventative and prescribed medicine in the future. The therapeutic benefits of nature offer a simple and cost-effective method for wellbeing. If this is coupled with impactful coaching and a behavioural change towards protecting our planet, then there's an efficient and impactful win all round. The holy grail!

While growing from a small base, large growth is to be expected, but I believe the interest in this field and the number of practitioners will supersede growth in any other area of coaching over the next 10 years.

ROI/Research

I spoke about ROI in relation to general coaching; if we ever needed any proof of the benefit of being outside, Covid-19 has done that for us in spades:

fresh air, germ safety, plenty of physical space, mental wellbeing having been prioritised further and people having experienced the benefits of nature first hand as they spent more time outdoors in lockdowns. We are pushing on an open door taking our conversations outside. It is likely, however, that as coaching outdoors grows, there will be a desire from stakeholders and coaches alike to understand just how much more effective and expansive the coaching is. I've spoken in this book about the benefits of creativity, perspective, short cuts to the heart of the matter and long-term change, to name a few, but as yet there is little robust research in this field to evidence this. It's an exciting time for the ROI of coaching outdoors vs indoors. I'm waiting with bated breath to see: Who will do the research? Is it client research? Coach research? Organisation research? Or all three? What metrics will be used? And what metrics matter to clients, coaches, stakeholders and organisations? One thing is certain, as more coaches take their practice outside and develop their own ways of incorporating nature into their work, we will see a rise in valuable research, case studies and more fully articulated theories and models. I can't wait.

Contribute

- If you are passionate about coaching outdoors, contribute to the profession's credentials by instigating or taking part in some research.

Conclusion

People spend their lives increasingly indoors. About 80% of Japan's population live in urban areas, and the average American now spends more than 90% of their time indoors. But we are designed to be connected to the natural world, to listen to the wind and taste the air.

Dr Qing Li, 2018, p.12

In the course of researching and writing this book, I have become even more passionate about my belief in the benefits of coaching outdoors. I have immersed myself in coaching outdoors in every way: with my clients, trawling the internet, investigating closely related topics, engaging in personal reflection, speaking to other coaches, asking business stakeholders for their perspective on coaching outdoors, doing surveys and following up every lead even remotely connected to coaching outdoors that people gave me. The process energised me and convinced me more at each turn that not only was there huge value in coaching outdoors, but that there was also huge value in writing this book as a resource to support others taking their coaching conversations outside.

I have established the compelling benefits of coaching outdoors for the coach, the client, the planet and the organisation. That there is an opportunity for being outside walking and talking to become more mainstream and less niche.

I strongly believe that all coaching education programmes should include coaching outdoors as part of the curriculum. And that leadership programmes should pay attention to the value gained from spending time in nature alone and with colleagues.

While coaching outdoors is not for everyone, it is appropriate for most and accessible for many. I hope that you have enjoyed and found value in this book and that you will either step outside for the first time or collaborate more extensively with nature in your coaching practice as a result of what you've read.

A final thought. Nature is rich with stimuli and the opportunity to connect at a somatic and soulful level; to listen to nature and our bodies. This brings possibilities for coaching, wellbeing and environmental connection. All this is missed if we stay indoors with our phones, central heating and laptops. While it may seem simple to step outside, my experience is that people often don't. By inviting people to do so, we are giving them the permission and catalyst they need to have a break from the constant pull of technology and meetings. To have an enriching experience in all senses and to help them unlock their potential.

The key message is that working with nature connects us and our clients with the natural world that we have evolved from and offers a phenomenal resource. Both in terms of what it can offer us, but also how, as we reignite that ancient integral connection, we get closer to the possibility of bringing about a change in how we look after our planet for the generations to come.

Appendices

Appendix 1

CoachingOutdoors.com

IF YOU WOULD like to stay connected and keep up to date with the latest news you can find us at www.coachingoutdoors.com

The mission of CoachingOutdoors.com is to make coaching outdoors as accessible as possible to as many people as possible. To provide a stimulating experience for professional and personal growth and wellbeing.

Coaching Outdoors is dedicated to providing: coaching, EMCC award-winning CPD programmes, team development, retreats and resources.

Our coaches are all EMCC or ICF accredited, attend regular supervision and are passionate and experienced in involving nature in the coaching relationship. They are all available for chemistry sessions and are geographically spread to cover most areas in the UK.

We run two **EMCC award-winning programmes**:

- *Getting Started Coaching Outdoors* is for coaches or line managers who would like to begin the journey of taking their coaching conversations outdoors. The programme runs virtually, part time over two weeks and includes time outdoors in the participants' local area. It provides the foundation for safe, mutual and accessible outdoor conversations, as well as offering a personal development journey for the participants.

- *Nature as Co-Facilitator* is for experienced coaches who already work outdoors. The programme supports coaches to develop a deeper practice with nature, both personally and professionally, and to invite nature into their coaching relationship at a deeper level. It is a two-week, part-time, virtual programme involving time outdoors in the coach's local area.

While the programmes are designed to equip people to coach outdoors, there are two further elements to them – wellbeing and nature connection – making these programmes multi-faceted and very rich in their offer.

Truly experiential learning from the programme; it far exceeded my expectations both for developing my coaching practice along with developing and nurturing me. I loved the variety of learning aids and thought-provoking journal questions, all bound up by beautiful images. The cohort gently keeping everyone accountable and the Zoom touchpoints added to connection and shared learning. I feel I can move my practice from coaching outdoors to collaborating with nature as a co-facilitator. I have so many more tools, ideas and approaches that I can now draw upon in service of my clients. Thank you! – Course Participant

We also run a **Wilderness Retreat** based in Scotland. Each retreat is bespoke to the individuals and the group at the time. The retreat is designed to take you away from the day-to-day pressures, offer perspective and help you focus on what really matters to you. If you like a bit of magic that you can't quite put your finger on, or one of those experiences that you struggle to articulate to people who weren't there then this is for you.

Lesley Roberts works both in the UK and internationally. She collaborates with organisations and leaders to support them in their organisation or team development journeys. She both consults and delivers on interventions that drive long-lasting high performance.

I want to say a very big thanks to you for your excellent preparation and engaging facilitation of the team and me :-), as well as your positive approach, and commitment to help us move forward at pace on our journey. The team are fully engaged in the work that is needed to drive our High Performance Collaboration journey. The conditions you've created and the focus you provide are a big reason for that. Look forward to the next chapter. – R. Carrol, VP Marketing, Wrigley

Appendix 2

Sample Risk Assessment Form

Clear Focus Coaching & Development - Coaching Outdoors

CLEAR FOCUS
COACHING AND DEVELOPMENT

What/When/Who is this Risk Management Plan for?	Sam Eddleston, Clear Focus Coaching & Development coaches clients (1:1) whilst walking outdoors. This is completed in public areas, such as local parks which may be local to Leamington Spa, or further afield. Affected persons: Client, Coach, and members of the public.
General Comments	Key hazards are related to COVID. In terms of terrain, we will be walking a short to moderate distance (3-4km in 60-90mins), at a slow pace. We are on public paths, mostly on well maintained routes.
Who is responsible for its completion?	Sam Eddleston, Owner, Clear Focus Coaching & Development
When was this?	This version was completed on 15th May 2022
Who reviewed it? When?	Simon Eddleston, NEBOSH on 15th May 2022
Is it subject to periodic review? If so, what is the frequency, when is the next review, and who will review it?	Yes, reviewed 6 monthly. Next review due: 15th November 2022
Who are the risk owners?	Some risk elements are owned by individuals e.g. coachee/client for medical disclosure/medication and complying with safety advice provided by coach. Otherwise, Sam Eddleston owns the risks described in this plan.

Risk Assessment System

Severity Rating (S)	Likelihood Rating (L)
1. Insignificant. No injury.	1. Rare. May occur in exceptional circumstances.
2. Minor. First aid only.	2. Unlikely. Will seldom occur.
3. Moderate. Hospital treatment required.	3. Possible. May occur.
4. Significant. Permanent disability. Fatal.	4. Probable. Will often occur.
5. Catastrophic. Multiple fatalities and hospitalisation of casualties.	5. Highly probable. Nearly certain.

Severity					
5	5	10	15	20	25
4	4	8	12	16	20
3	3	6	9	12	15
2	2	4	6	8	10
1	1	2	3	4	5
X	1	2	3	4	5
			Likelihood		

			Clear Focus - Coaching Outdoors Risk Assessment						
Risk ID	Hazard and Risk Description	Who is affected?	Controls in place	Severity	Likelihood	Risk Value (with existing controls)	Existing controls enough?	Additional controls needed? Who, where, when etc.	Prospective residual Risk Value
1	Risk of infection from Covid 19	Client and Coach	OWNER: Sam Eddleston Pre-event advice regarding declarations to be made and to bring face mask, hand sanitizer Briefing/declarations at start of event Compliance with publicly signed venue instructions Hand sanitizer, wipes (provided by 8am) Social distancing If Client starts to display symptoms, keep socially distanced and walk them back to their vehicle. If well enough, self-drive home.	2	2	4	Yes	Review in the event of new Government public health guidance	2
2	Risk of injury from slips, trips, and falls.	Client and Coach	OWNER: Sam Eddleston Pre-event advice regarding footwear. Pre-event weather check, and GO/NO-GO/MODIFY decision made to maximise safety. Briefing at start of walk to highlight any heightened route risks (e.g. due to weather). Remain on the well maintained footpaths and roads. In event of injury, apply first aid. Walk them to vehicle if slight injury and ensure they get home safely. Call emergency services if serious injury.	2	2	4	Yes	To be reviewed in light of weather	2
3	Risk of infection from pathogens: e.g. Lyme Disease (lyme borreliosis), Ticks	Client and Coach	OWNER: Sam Eddleston Remain well covered: good footwear, socks, long trousers. Tend towards permitted areas, reduce time on uncultivated heavily grassed and wooded areas bemore areas in southern and Northern England and the Scottish Highlands are higher risk areas). Rinse/wash hands, or use anti-bac wipes at end of walk.	3	1	3	Yes	To be reviewed in light of location/weather	3
4	Risk of injury arising from vehicle accident.	Client and Coach	OWNER: Sam Eddleston Normal vigilance by coach and client around parking area Choose well lit accessible parking locations Research routes in advance and choose safest place to park	3	2	6	Yes	Coach arrive early and advise of any unusual congestion by phone	3
5	Effect of cold from sudden adverse change in weather conditions.	Client and Coach	OWNER: Sam Eddleston Review weather forecast in advance and choose appropriate clothing advice, footwear. Defer event if not appropriate. Defer event if not appropriate Briefing at start of session, and check kit in light of weather.	2	2	4	Yes	To be reviewed in light of weather	2
6	Individuals with pre-existing medical conditions fail to manage themselves effectively and become ill.	Client	Seek medical disclosure as part of pre-event engagement. Including emergency contact numbers Monitoring by coach during the session. Individual to be encouraged to medicate, otherwise first aid and arrange evacuation by ambulance as necessary.	2	2	4	Yes		4
7	Risk of injury from insect stings and bites.	Client and Coach	OWNER: Sam Eddleston Seek disclosure as part of pre-event engagement and briefing at start Monitoring by coach during the session. Treatment (antican for plants & insects), first aid	4	4	4	Yes		4
8	Thirst / hunger.	Client and Coach	OWNER: Sam Eddleston In warm weather, coach recommends that client brings a water bottle Food and water carried by Coach	2	1	2	Yes	To be reviewed in light of weather	2
9	Risk of attack from 3rd party in public place or from lone working / meeting with stranger.	Coach	OWNER: Sam Eddleston Pre-event registration and referral of client from client company Remain visible in public place Keep record with third party of where going, with whom and duration Keep personal alarm and mobile phone on person	3	1	3	Yes		3

Appendix 3

Resources

HERE IS A little list of other sources of information about coaching outdoors that you might find useful. I imagine this list will expand rapidly over the coming few years.

Coaching Outdoors CPD Programmes

www.coachingoutdoors.com offering EMCC award-winning innovative CPD programmes and a personal development retreat.

- *Getting Started Coaching Outdoors* is a virtual, 10-day, part-time programme for line managers and coaches. It includes time in nature in your own geography.
- *Nature as Co-Facilitator* is designed for experienced coaches who already take some conversations outside. It is a virtual, 10-day, part-time programme. It includes time in nature in your own geography.
- *Wilderness Scotland Retreat* is open to all who would like to experience personal development in the wilds of nature.
- Masterclasses with guest experts, taking a deep dive into a variety of coaching outdoor topics.

Podcasts

www.coaching-outdoors.com – A podcast series hosted by Alex Burn and Anna-Marie Watson with guests from the world of coaching sharing their thoughts on coaching outdoors.

https://daregreatlycoaching.com/introducing-the-daring-self-leader-ship-podcast/ – Gerdi Verwoert talks to leaders, coaches and interesting people who have a connection with nature about self-leadership.

Ted Talk

www.youtube.com/watch?v=EBwuk0BlWMY – 'Letting nature be your coach' by James Farell and Dianna Tedoldi. The first Ted Talk to feature coaching and nature. I love the self-coaching exercise at the end.

Outdoor Leadership Qualifications

www.mountain-training.org is a great place to start your search if you'd like some outdoor guiding qualifications or to find guides who can support your events.

Questing

www.wildrites.uk – For those who have an interest in personal quests in nature. Take a look at what John and Alex offer.

Books

Hutchins, G. (2022). *Leading by Nature: The Process of Becoming a Regenerative Leader*. Tunbridge Wells: Wordzworth.

A handbook for regenerative leadership for leaders who care about the environment.

Long, S. (2014). *Hillwalking: The Official Handbook of the Mountain Training Walking Schemes*. Betws-y-Coed: Mountain Training UK.

Steve is an instructor at the Welsh National Mountain centre and the book is regularly updated.

Acknowledgements

Forget not that the earth delights to feel your bare feet and the winds long to play with your hair.

Khalil Gibran, 1931

I OFTEN WONDER who reads this bit in books. I know I rarely do. But, now being in the position to say thank you, I realise how important it is to the author to be able to acknowledge the support they have had along the way, for a book is not a one-person endeavour but the culmination of a journey that many have contributed to.

I am hugely grateful to all who have helped in the creation of this book. Without you, all of this would still be thoughts in my head. Alison Jones from Practical Inspiration Publishing, you are the catalyst for all of this. Your 10-day book challenge drew me in, made me believe I could do it, that there was value in what I had to offer, and set me on my way with a great foundation, which made the writing fairly easy. Your team of editors and experts have brought the polish and sparkle. Fi Macmillan, when I stalled for various reasons, you were my biggest supporter. Your unfaltering belief that I was the person best qualified to write this book is the thing that kept me going. I can still hear you now: *'It's your book to write.'*

To Billy Desmond and Charlotte Sills, who took an active interest in my MSc research into coaching outdoors when others were trying to dissuade me from the topic: thank you. You were the chink of light I needed when others were trying to close the door.

A big debt of thank you to all the clients, Coaching Outdoors course participants and colleagues who have walked alongside me in this work. Your shared stories, learnings, teachings and passion have developed me, and in turn the value that this book offers to others. In particular, Simon Hawtrey-Woore for role modelling a 100% outdoor practice; Sam Eddleston for continued pursuit of learning, sharing insights and raising the bar; Clare Burgum and Vince Kearney for our colleague supervision walks outdoors; and Clare Sheldon for your interest, passion, humour and spirit. And those 2020 Coaching Outdoors programme participants who nominated my work to the EMCC for a global award. Winning that award gave me the confidence that I was adding value to the coaching world.

To Emma Evison, Rob Moffet, Sarah Newitt, John Studdert-Kennedy, Richard Martin and all at Mars who invested in my development throughout my career there. Mars Inc, you offer such a great place to work and are gold standard at developing your associates. #proudlymars.

Not forgetting the leaders who trusted me, years before coaching outdoors was topical, and believed in the benefit of taking your teams to rural locations. You demonstrated that this work is relevant and immensely valuable to the corporate world: Martin Porter, Wayne Tessier, Ben Thompson, Neil Reynolds, Rachel Kelley, Rankin Carroll and Matt Bowler-Jones. You led the way, opening the door for others to follow with their teams. And each time I learnt something new, adding to the value I offered the next team.

Sue Knight, you set me on my way in this journey through the NLP training I attended with you. You are one of my strongest role models and I take you as my 'evoked-companion' into many coaching interventions. Without you, I would not be doing what I am today.

Phil Damant (1969–2003), philosopher and subtle coach. Our conversations on that mountaineering trip to Glenn Coe in 1994 were the seeds of so much. Thank you.

A debt of thanks to the people in my life who have been the background support team. The friends who have cheered me on, especially Laurianne Walsh who empowers me in so many ways, my colleague Sam Clarke who is always there delivering over and above; and Bazza (Barry Chamberlain), my biggest cheerleader in life. To my family, Rich and Torrin, who have managed around me while I've beavered away, and my Dad. 'Daddykins', you stand proudly by while I get on with my latest adventure. You offer the occasional note of appropriate caution then let me fly.

Finally, of course to Mother Nature. For all that you are and all you silently offer.

References

Abram, D. (1996). *The Spell of the Sensuous: Perception and Language in a More-Than-Human World*. New York: Pantheon Books.

Ackerman, C. E. (2020). What is Kaplan's Attention Restoration Theory (ART)? *PositivePsychology.com*. Available from https://positivepsychology.com/attention-restoration-theory/ [accessed 18 July 2022].

Albert, C., Aronson, J., Fürst, C. & Opdam, P. (2014). Integrating ecosystem services in landscape planning: Requirements, approaches, and impacts. *Landscape Ecology, 29*, 1277–1285.

Allen, R. (2020). Outdoor counselling in Derbyshire. *Ramblings*, hosted by Clare Balding. BBC Sounds. Available from www.bbc.co.uk/programmes/m000g3g5 [accessed 18 July 2022].

Allen, R. (2021). *Grounded: How Connection with Nature Can Improve Our Mental and Physical Wellbeing*. London: Mortimer Books.

Aquafolium (no date). What is the evidence? Available from https://aquafolium.co.uk/research/ [accessed 18 July 2022].

Atchley, R. A., Strayer, D. L. & Atchley, P. (2012). Creativity in the wild: Improving creative reasoning through immersion in natural settings. *PLoS One, 7*(12), e51474.

Attenborough, D. (2009). *How many people can live on Planet Earth?* [documentary]. Horizon, BBC.

Barrow, G. & Marshall, H. (2020). Ecological transactional analysis: Principles for a new movement. *The Transactional Analyst, 10*(2), 5–8.

Barton, J. & Pretty, J. (2010). What is the best dose of nature and green exercise for improving mental health? A multi-study analysis. *Environmental Science and Technology*, *44*(10), 3947–3955.

Bergen, T., Engelen, A. & Derksen, K. (2006). The quality of coaching in relation to the professional development of teachers. In F. K. Oser, F. Achtenhagen & U. Renold (eds), *Competence Oriented Teacher Training: Old Research Demands and New Pathways* (pp.97–114). Rotterdam: Sense.

Berger, R. (2007). Choosing the right space to work in: Reflections prior to a nature therapy session. *Australian Journal of Outdoor Education*, *11*(1), 41–45.

Berger, R. (2009). Being in nature: An innovative framework for incorporating nature in therapy with older adults. *Journal of Holistic Nursing*, *27*(1), 45–50.

Berger, R. & McLeod, J. (2006). Incorporating nature into therapy: A framework for practice. *Journal of Systemic Therapies*, *25*(2), 80–94.

Beringer, A. & Martin, P. (2003). On adventure therapy and the natural worlds: Respect nature's healing. *Journal of Adventure Education and Outdoor Learning*, *3*(1), 29–40.

Berman, M., Kross, E., Krpan, K., Askren, M., Burson, A., Deldin, P., Kaplan, S., Sherdell, L., Gotlib, I. & Jonides, J. (2012). Interacting with nature improves cognition and affect for individuals with depression. *Journal of Affective Disorders*, *140*(3), 300–305.

Berne, E. (1964). *Games People Play: A Psychology of Human Relationships*. London: Penguin Books.

Buber, M. (1923). *I and Thou*. Translated from German by W. Kaufmann, 2008. New York: Touchstone.

Carter, S. E., Draijer, R., Holder, S. M., Brown, L., Thijssen, D. H. & Hopkins, N. D. (2018). Regular walking breaks prevent the decline in cerebral blood flow associated with prolonged sitting. *Journal of Applied Physiology*, *125*(3), 790–798.

Catalyst 14. (2019). Coaching outdoors webinar. Available from www.youtube.com/watch?v=-c8u7CKgebI [accessed 18 July 2022].

Chief of the Suamisu Tribe (1854). Available from https://en.wikipedia.org/wiki/Chief_Seattle%27s_speech [accessed 26 September 2022].

Chouinard, Y. (2016). *Let My People Go Surfing: The Education of a Reluctant Businessman.* New York: Penguin Books.

Clarkson, P. (2000). *The Therapeutic Relationship.* London: Whurr Publishers.

Cluett, C. (2020). Coaching model: A seasonal approach to coaching. *ICA Blog,* 24 May 2020. Available from https://coachcampus.com/coach-port-folios/coaching-models/colleen-cluett-a-seasonal-approach-to-coaching [accessed 18 July 2022].

Cook, S. & van Nieuwerburgh, C. (2020). The experience of coaching whilst walking: A pilot study. *The Coaching Psychologist, 16*(2), 46–56.

Cormack, A., McRobert, L., Richardson, M. & Underhill, R. (2016). 30 Days Wild: Development and evaluation of a large-scale nature engagement campaign to improve well-being. *PLoS One, 11*(2): e0149777.

Crumley, J. (2020). Wild about Scotland nature expert Jim Crumley visits an old haunt and enjoys whispers in the woods. *The Scots Magazine,* 16 January 2020.

de Haan, E. (2008). *Relational Coaching: Journeys Towards Mastering One-to-One Learning.* Chichester: Wiley & Sons Ltd.

Einstein, A. (1950). Letter of condolence sent to Robert J. Marcus of the World Jewish Congress (12 February 1950). Quoted in *The New York Times,* 29 March 1972.

Fromm, E. (1973). *The Anatomy of Human Destructiveness.* London: Penguin Books.

Gendlin, E. T. (1982). *Focusing.* New York: Bantam Books.

Gidlow, C., Randall, J., Gillman, J., Smith, G. & Jones, M. (2016). Natural environments and chronic stress measured by hair cortisol. *Landscape and Urban Planning, 148,* 61–67.

Gladwell, V. F., Brown, D. K., Wood, C., Sandercock, G. R. & Barton, J. L. (2013). The great outdoors: How a green exercise environment can benefit all. *Extreme Physiology & Medicine, 2*(3), 1–7.

Grinde, B. & Patil, G. G. (2009). Biophilia: Does visual contact with nature impact on health and well-being? *International Journal of Environmental Research and Public Health, 6*(9), 2332–2343.

Hall, C. (2015). *Mindfulness-Based Ecotherapy: A 12 Session Programme for Reconnecting with Nature*. Mindfulness-Based Family Therapy.

Hawkins, P. (2020). Coaching in a changing climate webinar. Available from www.youtube.com/watch?v=_lTIcujMI4s [accessed 18 July 2022].

Hoban, J. (2019). *Walk with your Wolf: Unlock Your Intuition, Confidence and Power.* London: Yellow Kite.

Hodgkinson, G. P., Sadler-Smith, E., Burke, L., Claxton, G. & Sparrow, P. R. (2009). Intuition in organisations: Implications for strategic management. *Long Range Planning, 42*(3), 277–297.

Holland, C. (2014). *I Love My World: The Playful, Hands-on Nature Connections and Forest School Guidebook*. Devon: Wholeland Press, e-edition.

Hutchins, G. & Storm, L. (2019). Regenerative Leadership: The DNA of Life-Affirming 21st Century Organisations. Tunbridge Wells: Wordzworth Publishing.

International Coaching Federation (ICF) (2016). *2016 ICF Global Coaching Study*. Available from https://coachfederation.org/app/uploads/2017/12/2016ICFGlobalCoachingStudy_ExecutiveSummary-2.pdf [accessed 18 July 2022].

International Coaching Federation (ICF) (2018). The gift of coaching presence. Available from https://coachingfederation.org/blog/gift-coaching-presence [accessed 18 July 2022].

International Coaching Federation (ICF) (2019). *Leading Boldly: 2019 Annual Report*. Available from https://coachingfederation.org/app/uploads/2020/11/ICF_2019_AnnualReport.pdf [accessed 18 July 2022].

International Coaching Federation (ICF) (2020). *2020 ICF Global Coaching Study*. Available from https://coachingfederation.org/app/uploads/2020/09/FINAL_ICF_GCS2020_ExecutiveSummary.pdf [accessed 18 July 2022].

International Coaching Federation (ICF) (2021). COVID-19 and the Coaching Industry: 2021 ICF Global Snapshot Survey Results. Study commissioned by the ICF and undertaken by PwC. Available from https://coachingfederation.org/app/uploads/2021/05/2021ICF_COVIDStudy_Part2_FINAL.pdf?inf_contact_key=f1de0c67eb7ec1bf44c6c67e0cf52bb-11b0a3f0fd3ee5d9b43fb34c6613498d7 [accessed 18 July 2022].

International Coaching Federation (ICF) (2022). #ExperienceCoaching. Available from https://coachingfederation.org/find-a-coach-1/experience-coaching [accessed 18 July 2022].

Jonides, J., Lewis, R. L., Nee, D. E., Lustig, C. A., Berman, M. G. & Moore, K. S. (2008). The mind and brain of short-term memory. *Annual Review of Psychology, 59*, 193–224.

Kaplan, S. (1995). The restorative benefits of nature: Toward an integrative framework. *Journal of Environmental Psychology, 15*(3), 169–182.

Kaplan, R. & Kaplan, S. (1989). *The Experience of Nature: A Psychological Perspective.* New York: Cambridge University Press.

Kaplan, S. & Berman, M. G. (2010). Directed attention as a common resource for executive functioning and self-regulation. *Perspectives on Psychological Science, 5*(1), 43–57.

Kellert, S. R. & Wilson, E. O. (1995). *The Biophilia Hypothesis.* Washington, DC: Island Press.

Kilburg, R. (2004). Trudging toward Dodoville: Conceptual approaches and case studies in executive coaching. *Consulting Psychology Journal: Practice and Research, 56*(4), 203–213.

King, K. (2012). The challenge of mutuality. In E. de Haan & C. Sills (eds), *Coaching Relationships: The Relational Coaching Field Book* (pp.55–56). Faringdon: Libri Publishing.

Klepeis, N. E., Nelson, W. C., Ott, W. R., Robinson, J. P., Tsang, A. M., Switzer, P., Behar, J. V., Hern, S. C. & Engelmann, W. H. (2001). The national human activity pattern survey (NHAPS): A resource for assessing exposure to environmental pollutants. *Journal of Exposure Science and Environmental Epidemiology, 11*(3), 231–252.

Knight, S. (1995). *NLP at Work: The Difference That Makes a Difference in Business.* London: Nicholas Brealey Publishing.

Kolb, D. A. (1984). *Experiential Learning: Experience as the Source of Learning and Development.* Englewood Cliffs, NJ: Prentice Hall.

Leary-Joyce, J. (2014). *The Fertile Void: Gestalt Coaching at Work.* St Albans: AoEC Press.

Lewis, T., Amini, F. and Lannon, R. (2000). *A General Theory of Love*. New York: Random House.

Li, Q. (2018). *Shinrin-Yoku: The Art and Science of Forest Bathing*. London: Penguin UK.

Liebenguth, K. (2015). Let's get outside. *Coaching at Work, 10*(3). Available from www.coaching-at-work.com/2015/04/11/lets-get-outside [accessed 18 July 2022].

Lightfoot, L. (2019). Forest schools: Is yours more a marketing gimmick than an outdoors education? *The Guardian*, 25 June 2019. Available from www.theguardian.com/education/2019/jun/25/forest-schools-more-mar-keting-than-outdoor-education [accessed 18 July 2022].

Macfarlane, R. (2008). *Mountains of the Mind: A History of a Fascination*. London: Granta Books.

Mackay, C. M. L. & Schmitt, M. T. (2019). Do people who feel connected to nature do more to protect it? A meta-analysis. *Journal of Environmental Psychology, 65*, 101323.

Marshall, H. (2016). Taking therapy outside – Reaching for a vital connection. Keynote Presentation at *CONFER Conference, Psychotherapy & the Natural World*, 12–13 November 2016.

McGeeney, A. (2016). *With Nature in Mind: The Ecotherapy Manual for Mental Health Professionals*. London: Jessica Kingsley Publishers.

Meikle, J. (2016). Antidepressant prescriptions in England double in a decade. *The Guardian*, 5 July 2016. Available from www.theguardian.com/society/2016/jul/05/antidepressant-prescriptions-in-england-dou-ble-in-a-decade [accessed 18 July 2022].

Natural England (2022). Social prescribing: The power of nature as treatment. Available from https://naturalengland.blog.gov.uk/2022/04/12/social-pre-scribing-the-power-of-nature-as-treatment/ [accessed 18 July 2022].

Newell, D. (2015). Setting up coaching for success by questioning more in contracting. *Coach & Mentor, the OCM Journal, 15*, 2–5.

O'Broin, A. & Palmer, S. (2006). Reappraising the coach-client relationship. In S. Palmer & A. Whybrow (eds), *Handbook of Coaching Psychology: A Guide for Practitioners* (pp.295–324). London: Routledge.

O'Donovan, H. (2015). *Mindful Walking: Walk Your Way to Mental and Physical Well-being.* London: Hachette UK Ltd.

O'Mara, S. (2019). *In Praise of Walking: The New Science of How We Walk and Why It's Good for Us.* London: Bodley Head.

O'Riordan, S. & Palmer, S. (2019). Beyond the coaching room into blue space: Ecopsycholology informed coaching psychology practice. *Journal of Psychology International, 12*(1), 8–18.

Ogden, P., Minton, K. & Pain, C. (2006). *Trauma and the Body: A Sensorimotor Approach to Psychotherapy.* New York: W. W. Norton & Company.

Oppezzo, M. & Schwartz, D. L. (2014). Give your ideas some legs: The positive effect of walking on creative thinking. *Journal of Experimental Psychology: Learning, Memory, and Cognition, 40*(4), 1142–1152.

Oprah & Tolle, E. (2019). *A New Earth: Awakening to Your Life's Purpose.* Podcast series. Available from https://open.spotify.com/episode/3UvRpQz-VcbtMzApr2dWmdH [accessed 18 July 2022].

Palmer, W. & Crawford, S. (2013). *Leadership Embodiment: How the Way We Sit and Stand Can Change the Way We Think and Speak.* San Rafael, CA: Create Space.

Parsloe, E. (1999). *The Manager as Coach and Mentor.* London: CIPD.

Passmore, J. & Marianetti, O. (2007). The role of mindfulness in coaching. *The Coaching Psychologist, 3*(3), 131–137.

Roberts, J. L. (2016). *How Are We in Nature and How Does it Shape the Quality of Our Coaching Conversations?* MSc Dissertation, Ashridge Business School. Unpublished.

Rogers, C. R. (1961). *On Becoming a Person: A Therapist's View of Psychology.* London: Constable.

Roszak, T. (2001). *The Voice of the Earth: An Exploration of Ecopsychology.* Grand Rapids, MI: Phanes Press.

Rousseau, J. J. (1953). *The Confessions of Jean Jacques Rousseau,* trans. with an introduction by J. M. Cohen. Harmondsworth: Penguin.

St. Pierre, P. & Smith, M. (2014). Intuition in coaching: It's not magic. *Strategies: A Journal for Physical and Sports Educators, 27*(2), 37–42.

Salas, E., Rosen, M. A. & DiazGranados, D. (2010). Expert-based intuition and decision making in organisations. *Journal of Management, 36*(4), 941–973.

Saraev, V. & The Forestry Commission (2020). Valuing the mental health benefits of forestry – Phase 2. Available from www.forestresearch.gov.uk/research/valuing-the-mental-health-benefits-of-forestry-phase-2/ [accessed 18 July 2022].

Schein, E. H. & Bennis, Warren, G. (1965). *Personal and Organizational Change Through Group Methods: The Laboratory Approach.* New York: Wiley.

Schultz, P. W. (2002). Inclusion with nature: The psychology of human-nature relations. In P. Schmuck & P. W. Schultz (eds), *Psychology of Sustainable Development* (pp.61–78). Boston, MA: Springer.

Scott, K. (2017). *Radical Candor.* London: Macmillan.

Searles, H. F. (1955). The informational value of the supervisor's emotional experience. *Psychiatry, 18*(2), 135–146.

Seattle, N., Chief of the Suamisu Tribe (1854). *Chief Seattle's Response.*

Selhub, E. M. & Logan, A. C. (2014). *Your Brain on Nature: The Science of Nature's Influence on Your Health, Happiness and Vitality.* New York: Collins.

Sheldon, C. (2018). Trust your gut, listen to reason: How experienced coaches work with intuition in their practice. *International Coaching Psychology Review, 13*(1), 6–20.

Siegel, D. J. (1999). *The Developing Mind: Towards a Neurobiology of Interpersonal Experience.* New York: Guilford Press.

Sills, C. (2006). *Contracts in Counselling and Psychotherapy* (2nd ed.). London: Sage.

Silsbee, D. (2008). *Presence-Based Coaching: Cultivating Self-Generative Leaders Through Mind, Body, and Heart.* San Francisco, CA: Jossey-Bass.

Snyder, G. (1990). *The Practice of the Wild: Essays.* Albany, CA: North Point Press.

Sport England (2015). *Getting Active Outdoors: A Study of Demography, Motivation, Participation and Provision in Outdoor Sport and Recreation in England.* Available from https://sportengland-production-files.s3.eu-west-2.amazonaws.com/s3fs-public/outdoors-participation-report-v2-lr-spreads.pdf [accessed 18 July 2022].

Strozzi-Heckler, R. (2014). *The Art of Somatic Coaching: Embodying Skillful Action, Wisdom and Compassion*. Berkeley, CA: North Atlantic Books.

Totton, N. (2011). *Wild Therapy: Undomesticated Inner and Outer Worlds*. Monmouth: PCCS Books.

Totton, N. (2014). The practice of wild therapy. *Therapy Today, 25*(5), 14–17.

Tudor, K. (2011). Understanding empathy. *Transactional Analysis Journal, 41*(1), 39–57.

Turner, A. F. (2017). Coaching through walking. *The Coaching Psychologist, 13*(2), 80–87.

Ulrich, R. S. (1984). View through a window may influence recovery from surgery. *Science, 224*(4647), 420–421.

Wampold, B. (2001). *The Great Psychotherapy Debate: Models, Methods, and Findings*. Mahwah, NJ: Lawrence Erlbaum Inc.

Watts, A. (1973). *Cloud-Hidden, Whereabouts Unknown: A Mountain Journal*. New York: Vintage.

Weuve, J., Kang, J. H., Manson, J. E., Breteler, M. M. B., Ware, J. H. & Grodstein, F. (2004). Physical activity, including walking, and cognitive function in older women. *Jama, 292*(12), 1454–1461.

White, M. P., Alcock, I., Wheeler, B. W. & Depledge, M. H. (2013). Would you be happier living in a greener urban area? A fixed-effects analysis of panel data. *Psychological Science, 6*(6), 920–928.

Whitmore, J. (2002). *Coaching for Performance: Growing People, Performance and Purpose* (3rd ed.). London: Nicholas Brealey Publishing.

Wildflower, L. & Brennan, D. (eds) (2011). *The Handbook of Knowledge-Based Coaching: From Theory to Practice*. San Francisco, CA: Jossey-Bass.

World Health Organization (2021). *Green and Blue Spaces and Mental Health: New Evidence and Perspectives for Action*. Available from https://apps.who.int/iris/bitstream/handle/10665/342931/9789289055666-eng.pdf [accessed 18 July 2022].

Youell, R. (2019). Forest bathing: Shinrin-yoku. *The Transactional Analyst*, Autumn 2019, 17–22.

Index

accreditation 182
adventure therapy 10
Albert, C. 85
Allen, R. 32, 42, 130
antidepressants 18
anxiety rare 17–18
Aristotle 40
Attenborough, D. 49
attention restoration theory
    (ART) 41–42
Augustine, St 40
authenticity 58–59
autumn 147–149
awareness, multi-dimensional 125

beauty 32
becoming open 138–139
Bennis, W. G. 71
Berger, R. 10, 74, 75, 76, 124
Beringer, A. 9
Berne, E. 79
berries and leaves 149
Berry, W. 118
biodiversity loss 32
biophilia hypothesis 10, 41
blue spaces 11, 85
bravery 59–60, 68
Buber, M. 127

check in – check out 133
checklist
    for coaching outdoors 81
    for location 91
chemistry sessions 73–74, 172
Chouinard, Y. 64
Chronos time 142
clear thinking 48
client
    connection 54–56
    experiences 45–51
    supporting choices of 104–105
client session, planning for 78
Climate Coaching
    Alliance (CCA) 20
climate crisis 19–20, 32
clothing 99–100
coach experiences 53–60
coaching
    definitions of 3–5
    market growth 181–182
    and therapy, comparison 12–13
coaching outdoors (generally) 7–14
    checklist 81
    contributing to 186
    demand for 15–16
    reflection 107
    when not to 71–72

coaching presence 54–55
CoachingOutdoors.com 191–192
comfort zones 83–84, 93–96
compassion 32
confidentiality 81–82
congruence 58, 59
Conservation Volunteers,
    The (TCV) 39
constellation exercise 139–140
contracts 79
    agreeing 82
    areas of 79
    for coaching outdoors versus for
        normal coaching 80–81
    confidentiality 81–82
    initial conversation 80
    option for indoor sessions 81
    sessional 81
    for teams outdoors 162
Cook, S. 46–47, 49
corporate experience 182–183
Covid-19 pandemic, impact of 15,
    18–19, 35
creativity 48–50
    and walking, link between 40
Crumley, Jim 27
Csíkszentmihályi, M. 56

Davenport, H. 123
dawn chorus 145
de Haan, E. 5, 156
depression 17–18, 37
Dickens, C. 40

Earth
    coach's role in the environmental
        agenda 32
    and humans, relationship between
        26–28, 32
    and nature connectedness 30–32, 33
ecological transactional analysis (Eco-
    TA) 10–11

ecotherapy 10
Einstein, A. 29
emotion 32
European Mentoring and Coaching
    Council (EMCC) 182
evolution 25–26
executive coaching, definition of 3–4
experience reflection 61

'flow' 56–58, 157
footwear 100–101
forest bathing 11
forest schools 123–124
forests 75
Fromm, E. 41
future
    of coaching 181–184
    of coaching outdoors 185–186
future proof 184

Getting Started Coaching Outdoors
    programme 191
global trends 16
green gyms 39
green spaces 11, 85
groups
    being outdoors with 175
    and teams, difference between
        161–162

Hahn, K. 10
Hawkins, P. 19–20
Hawtrey-Woore, S. 175
healers, ancient 38
health conditions, of client 80
Hippocrates 39
Hoban, J. 75
Holland, C. 128, 162
Hutchins, G. 51

Inclusion of Nature in Self (INS)
    model 118–119

indoor virtual sessions 173–174
insurance and training 103–104
intention walk 176
International Coaching Federation
  (ICF) 182
intuition 26, 72–73, 155–157

Kairos time 142
Kaplan, R. 41, 42
Kaplan, S. 41, 42
Kellert, S. 41
King, K. 46, 75
kit 105
  bags 103
  first aid kit 103
  map 103
  pen and paper 102
  sit mat 103
  sunglasses 101
  water 101
Kolb, D. A. 87–88
Kövecses, Z. 129–130

landscapes 74, 86
leaders, demands on 16–17
learning cycle (Kolb) 87–88
learning tree 138
Leary-Joyce, J. 123
Lewis, T. 55
Li, Q. 11
Liebenguth, K. 46
Lightfoot, L. 123
location 75–77, 83
  checklist 91
  environment 84–85
  exploration 105
  exploring 90
  feeling right 89–90
  fundamental and logistical basics 87
  good location 85–87
  green/blue spaces 85
  physical comfort 83–84

portfolio of 89
regular 86–87
teams outdoors 163
and travel time 87–88
unknown venues 88–89
Logan, A. C. 38

Macfarlane, R. 24
Mackay, C. M. 30
Macmillan, F. 54, 116, 175
map creation 137–138
Marianetti, O. 58
Marshall, H. 28, 30, 124–125
Martin, P. 9
McGeeney, A. 23, 37, 47
McLean, J. 20
meaning 32
medicine walk 11
memory, and nature 42
mental health 38
Mental Health Foundation, UK 39
metaphors 129–135
mirror neurons 55
mirror/parallel process 135–137
  becoming open 138–139
  constellations 139–140
  learning tree 138
  map creation 137–138
multi-dimensional awareness 125

nature 7, 8–9, 23–25, 188
  commune with 118
  connectedness 30–32, 33
  feeling 147
  and mental health 37–38
  observation of 151
  positive effects of 36–38
  prescribing 38–39
  psychological theories 41–42
  remote coaching with 169–177
  rhythm of 141–142
  safe environment 60

as a silent partner 175
soft fascination in 42, 46
as a third party 124
and wellbeing 27
nature as a co-facilitator 128, 150
definition of 123–124
framing 125–126
with teams 163–164
Nature as Co-Facilitator programmes
77, 192
nature connectedness 65, 67, 111–114
practices 115–119
nature connection, between sessions
176–177
nature switch continuum 116, 117–
118
nature therapy 10
nature-based interventions 9–14
adventure therapy 10
blue/green coaching 11
ecological transactional analysis
(Eco-TA) 10–11
ecotherapy 10
medicine walk 11
nature therapy 10
questing interventions 11
Shinrin-Yoku/forest bathing 11
Vision Quest 11–12
walking therapy 10
wilderness therapy 9–10
Nelson, A. 37
Nietzsche, F. 40

O'Donovan, H. 47
O'Mara, S. 39, 48
Oppezzo, M. 40, 48–49
organisational benefits 63–68
O'Riordan, S. 39
outdoor virtual sessions 174–175
outdoors with groups, being 175
'Outward Bound' organisation 10
owl, as a sign 134

Palmer, S. 39
parallel process see mirror/parallel
process
Passmore, J. 58
past experiences 74–75
Pathways to Nature Connectedness
Framework 31
'Peace of Wild Things, The'
(poem) 118
person-centred approach (Rogers) 4
perspectives 50–51, 135
phone coaching 169–172
physical health 38–39
preparation ritual 61
priming between sessions 177
psychological safety 71, 72–73, 75, 77,
162
psychotherapy 12

quality organisational outputs 64
questing interventions 11

radical candour 67–68
regulations 182
relational coaching 4–5
remote coaching 169
creating a natural environment
inside 174
indoor virtual sessions 173–174
nature connection between sessions
176–177
outdoor virtual sessions 174–175
phone coaching 169–172
touchpoints between sessions 177
representation 133
resilience 65
results speed 66
return on investment 183, 185–186
rhythm of nature 141–142
Richardson, M. 37
Roberts, L. 86, 192–193
Rogers, C. R. 4, 58

Rousseau, J. J. 40
Rowland, M. 39

safe environment 75–77
Schein, E. H. 71
Schmitt, M. T. 30
Schultz, P. W. 118
Schwartz, D. L. 48–49
Scott, K. 68
Searles, H. F. 135–136
seasons 142–143, 153
    attributes 143
    autumn 147–149
    bringing inside 152
    spring 143–145
    summer 145–147
    winter 149–151
self-awareness 152
Selhub, E. M. 38
senses 31, 151–152
shamanism 10
Sheldon, C. 156
Shinrin-Yoku 11
side-by-side, being 46–47, 58–59, 77
signs 133–135
silence 47, 77
Silsbee, D. 54
Snyder, G. 27
society, current trends 17–18
specialisms, coaching 184
spring 143–145
Strayer, D. 9
stress 37
Strozzi-Heckler, R. 26
summer 145–147

'taking others along' 66–67
talk therapy 47
teams
    activity outdoors 165–167
    contracting and psychological safety
        162
    and groups, difference between
        161–162
    location choice 163
    nature as a co-facilitator with
        163–164
    reflections from participants 164–
        165
technology growth, impact of 24
therapy and coaching, comparison
    12–13
thinking, clarity of 48
thinking time 64
Totton, N. 74, 124, 127
transference 127
travel time 87–88
Turner, E. 20, 48

unexpected emotions, management of
    77–78
unknown venues 88–89

van Nieuwerburgh, C. 46–47, 49
virtual coaching 183
Vision Quest 11–12
visual metaphors 130

walking 140
    benefits of 39–40
    distance, in coaching outdoor 80
    intention walk 176
    medicine walk 11
    positive effects of 47, 48
    sensual seasonal walk 153
    side by side 55–56
    as therapy 10
walled garden 76
Watts, A. 23
weather 93, 97–98
    comfort zones 93–96, 98
    warm and sunny 97
    windy 96–97
wellbeing 35

experience 43
positive effects of nature 36–38
Weuve, J. 40
White, M. 65, 85
Whitmore, J. 4
Whybrow, A. 20

Wilderness Retreat 192
wilderness therapy 9–10
Wilson, E. O. 10, 41
winter 149–151

yellow bird, as a sign 134–135